Security Strategy of Intelligent Transport's Telematic Systems

This book is a monograph devoted to one of the key challenges of modern transport – the safety strategy for telematics systems being used in the movement of people and cargo. In this sense, the publication aligns with current research trends related to the dynamic development of information and telecommunications technologies which are shaping new operating models for transport and logistics companies.

The authors address issue of strategic transport management, focusing on the role of telematics as a tool supporting efficiency, automation, and coordination of operations. Particular emphasis is placed on the issues of risk and safety – which, in an era of growing transport volumes and intensifying competition in the transport market, are becoming a prerequisite for the reliability and sustainable development of the entire industry.

The book demonstrates that the safe use of telematics systems is not only a technological requirement, but also a social and environmental one. It is in line with European Union policy, which prioritizes environmental protection, improving social well-being, and reducing road accidents, which constitute one of the greatest threats to civilization.

Combining theoretical and practical perspectives, this monograph offers a comprehensive overview of the implementation of secure telematics solutions. It is a valuable resource for transport researchers and students, as well as for logistics company managers and decision-makers responsible for infrastructure development and transport policy.

Security Strategy of Intelligent Transport's Telematic Systems

Anna Brzozowska, Wojciech Dyduch,
Aleksander Pabian, Barbara Pabian and
Magdalena Sobocińska

CRC Press
Taylor & Francis Group
Boca Raton London New York

CRC Press is an imprint of the
Taylor & Francis Group, an **informa** business

Designed cover image: Shutterstock ID: 2603847321

First edition published 2026
by CRC Press
2385 NW Executive Center Drive, Suite 320, Boca Raton FL 33431

and by CRC Press
4 Park Square, Milton Park, Abingdon, Oxon, OX14 4RN

CRC Press is an imprint of Taylor & Francis Group, LLC

ISBN: 9781041078821 (hbk)
ISBN: 9781041086772 (pbk)
ISBN: 9781003646518 (ebk)

DOI: 10.1201/9781003646518

Typeset in Caslon
by Newgen Publishing UK

Contents

About the Authors

Anna Brzozowska is an associate professor in the field of economics, specializing in management sciences. She currently works at the Department of Logistics at the Faculty of Management, Częstochowa University of Technology. Her research and academic activities focus on management processes, particularly on the use of information and communication technologies in decision-making, logistics, and marketing. She is also interested in the institutional environment influencing organizational efficiency and development in the context of European integration. Her main scientific interests concern the application of information technologies in management and business, project management, including projects co-financed by the European Union, as well as management and marketing in agribusiness and the role of logistics and marketing as supporting elements of management processes. She continuously develops these areas through participation in national and international research projects, involvement in academic and R&D teams, and collaboration with businesses as well as local and regional authorities. She is the author or co-author of approximately 190 scientific publications, including monographs, book chapters, and articles in national and international journals. Her professional achievements also include participation in numerous implementation projects and active engagement in the development of young researchers and the promotion of science.

Wojciech Dyduch is currently vice-rector for education and international cooperation and the head of the Department of Entrepreneurship at the University of Economics in Katowice. He is also a member of the Council of Scientific Excellence and the chairman of the Committee of Organization and Management Sciences. Previously, he was vice-dean for didactics, then vice-rector for education as well as a vice-dean for development at the University of Economics in Katowice. Author and co-author of over 150 scientific publications, including books, among them entitled: "Creative strategy of the organization", Publishing House of the University of Economics in Katowice, Katowice 2014. The manager of several grants awarded by the National Science Center, he is mainly a researcher of strategic management and organizational entrepreneurship problems. Currently he mainly deals with the issues of creative projects in organizations, organizational effectiveness, creating and capturing values by entrepreneurial organizations, measuring organizational entrepreneurship.

Aleksander Pabian is an assistant professor at Częstochowa University of Technology, Częstochowa, Poland. He conducts there scientific activity focused mainly on management and logistics. It is focused both on following national and international achievements as well as on internationalizing his own scientific work. To this date, he has published two independent scientific monographs (another three in co-authorship). He is also the author or co-author of more than 70, other publications, including those published in prestigious scientific journals and peer-reviewed materials from international conferences, included in the list of the Minister of Education and Science, characterized by a high visibility index, indexed in the Science Citation Index Expanded, Web of Science, Scopus, and other databases. He has also participated in over 40 national and international scientific conferences, organized both in Poland and abroad.

Barbara Pabian is a professor at the University of Economics in Katowice. She is the author and co-author of approximately 150 scientific papers, including 8 books and articles, published in prestigious international journals. Her research interests include issues related to the implementation of the sustainable management concept into various industries and sectors of the economy. She co-organized and participated in multiple international conferences and student-doctoral seminars, being a member of their Program and Scientific Councils. She conducted international research activities and participated in ERASMUS+ academic exchange programmes (Turkey, Ukraine). She served as the dean of the Faculty of Tourism at the Hotel Management and Tourism High School in Częstochowa. She is a member of the Commission for the Acceptance of Scientific and Research Works in the discipline of Management Science and Quality. She serves as an expert of the National Institute of Rural Culture and Heritage in Warsaw. For her research activities, she has been honoured with numerous awards and grants from the Rector of the University of Economics in Katowice. For her activities in the field of teaching she was awarded the Medal of National Education.

Magdalena Sobocińska is an associate professor at Wroclaw University of Economics and Business. She specializes in issues related to the use of the new media in management and marketing, marketing research, consumption development processes, sustainable development, and the functioning of the cultural sphere. She is an author and co-author of over 230 publications in this field in the form of monographs, chapters in monographs and textbooks, and articles. She is a co-editor of eight issues of Scientific Papers of Wroclaw University of Economics and three monographs devoted to the issues of marketing research. She received the award of the Minister of Science and Higher Education for the doctoral dissertation. Her postdoctoral monograph was awarded in the competition for scientific works by the Committee on Organizational and Management of the Polish Academy of Sciences. She is a member of the Board at the Polish Scientific Marketing Society. She is also Rector's Representative for Cooperation with the Polish and Czech Association of Universities.

Introduction

A significant factor in economic development across all spatial scales, that is, local, regional, national, and global, is transportation. As a distinct sector of the economy, it encompasses activities related to the movement of people and the flow of goods. This means that various types of land, water, air, and specialized transportation are carried out within it. Researchers agree that the factors determining the efficient operation of transportation processes today include not only intelligent and eco-friendly means of transport, good infrastructure, appropriate legal regulations, effective logistics, and sustainable fleet management (from planning and execution to monitoring and control), but also, and perhaps above all, modern technologies. Modern telematics solutions and tools, which combine telecommunications with information technology, are already almost universally used globally.

Modern telematics systems operate based on stationary, mobile, or satellite telecommunications networks, including sensor networks. They utilize a variety of sensors, cameras, transmitters, and on-board diagnostics to monitor traffic, driving style, vehicle technical condition, and IT systems (hardware and software). Intelligent transport systems (ITS) represent today's most promising and effective solution. They contribute to the acceleration and improvement of communication potential. They significantly streamline transport processes, reducing travel time and increasing the safety of travel and freight transport as well as reducing the negative impact of transport on the environment.

However, the implementation of telematics systems for transportation brings new challenges stemming from the dynamic pace of telematics development. Initial solutions involved simple satellite monitoring systems aimed at preventing vehicle theft; today, we have technologically advanced tools supporting fleet management, such as complex platforms utilizing artificial intelligence and cloud computing. New challenges are constantly emerging. They are of a technical nature (e.g. regarding the integration of the telematics system with the remaining IT infrastructure or protection against malware

DOI: 10.1201/9781003646518-1

and man-in-the-middle-type attacks), legal nature, concerning the collection, processing, sharing, and protection of personal data, as well as psychological which is related to users' resistance, for example, to vehicle activity tracking.

With this in mind, the authors of this study attempt to synthesize the existing knowledge on the genesis, essence, potential, and development of intelligent transport telematics systems, focusing on their security strategy. This synthesis underscores the necessity of addressing technical, legal, and human factors in the development of intelligent transport telematics, ensuring that system design is robust, secure, and aligned with contemporary technological standards.

The main objective of the monograph is to present the current state of knowledge on the integrated application of the latest technologies and management strategies in transport and, on this background, to provide specific recommendations and guidelines which, if implemented, will lead to sustainable and safe fleet management as well as to increase the safety and efficiency of transport operations while simultaneously caring for the natural environment. The substantive content has been selected and synthesized in a methodical manner by a professional team of scientists.

In accordance with the adopted substantive and methodological assumptions, Chapter 1 discusses the issue of strategy in transport management. It emphasizes the importance of the strategic paradigm, which is applicable to transport management, both from the macroeconomic perspective of the state and the microeconomic perspective of individual transport companies. The multiplicity of ways of interpreting the concept of strategy has also been pointed out, which results from various epistemological, axiological, and methodological assumptions adopted by various researchers.

The considerations presented in the next, second chapter highlight the complex systemic nature of intelligent transport, which requires the balanced integration of all its elements: means of transport, infrastructure, technologies as well as responsible, sustainable management. Among other things, the main types and modes of transport are discussed, linear and point infrastructure is characterized and it is placed in the context of the importance of technological innovations in the development of tomorrow's mobility.

Another important part of the monograph is the third chapter, which has a theoretical dimension. It expertly presents the state of the art in the topic of telematics systems. It further clarifies the modularity, interoperability, and scalability of telematics, which determine the efficiency, safety, sustainability as well as strategic management of transport companies. A complement of the whole is a compelling fourth chapter, which focuses on security standards, presenting them in the context of key risk categories. They are presented in an updated form of the existing cybersecurity landscape.

In summary, the book addresses a very important and current social issue. Its content aligns with the latest research trends related to the dynamic development of information systems and new technologies, without which the development of businesses, not only those in transportation, will be hampered. Thanks to the thoughtful selection of content, the monograph provides synthesized and up-to-date knowledge on the issues being discussed. Reading it will help readers not only to recognize the challenges that arise or may arise in connection with the dynamic development of intelligent transport, but also provide specific, practical recommendations regarding, among others, organizational design, technical safety, monitoring and improvement as well as sustainable management of the transport and logistics sector. The authors demonstrated that, despite numerous threats and weaknesses, implementing intelligent transportation systems is cost-effective and will positively impact transportation development. It is also worth emphasizing that the considerations and research findings regarding telematics can be adapted to other sectors of the economy.

The authors of this monograph direct it to all those interested in the discussed issues, and in particular to people and entities specializing in the development of security of telecommunications and IT solutions – hardware and software collecting data for modern transport. The monograph will be useful to business practitioners, academic staff, and students, awakening their need to think creatively and innovatively in the spirit of corporate social responsibility.

The authors hope that this study will be an inspiration for further scientific discussion and empirical research, translating into specific solutions that, when implemented in practice, will improve the discussed branch of the economy, i.e. transport. They also believe that the presented reflections will contribute to building a deeper understanding of the relationship between technological innovation, management efficiency, and safety in transport systems. In the long term, such considerations may support the development of sustainable and intelligent transport networks, aligned with the needs of a modern, dynamically changing society.

1
Strategy in Transport Management

1.1 Concept of Strategy

Transport, which performs many important functions from the point of view of the economy and meeting the needs of its users, is subject to transformations that are a consequence of globalization processes, the influence of the state and transport policy, changes in the behaviour of transport users, and the implementation of management concepts and methods in the sphere of transport.

The competitiveness of transport companies is affected by speed, flexibility, reliability, and security of supply, and competition takes an intra- and inter-industry character.

The complexity of the market in which transport companies operate is expressed, among others, in the fact that, apart from individual customers, there are also institutional buyers i.e. manufacturers, intermediaries, non-profit organizations, state administration entities on this market. These entities are more often and to a greater extent guided by specifications and technical data when choosing an offer, as well as the provided services and their range. At the same time, it should be noted that in the case of institutional customers, decisions on the selection of a transport company are often made by a multi-person decision-making centre through negotiations. In addition, on the B2B market, there is individualization of marketing activities in the scope of most elements that are subject to negotiation (Kotler, Pfoertsch, 2008, pp. 29–37; Wojciechowski, 2003, p. 21).

The strategic paradigm is an important paradigm that finds application in transport management, both from the macro perspective – the state and the micro perspective – individual transport companies.

DOI: 10.1201/9781003646518-2

Strategy, which has its roots in ancient military thought, is defined in several ways, depending on what, according to individual authors, constitutes the core of strategy. Various ways of interpreting strategies result from the researchers' adoption of different epistemological, axiological and methodological assumptions (Chybalski, Zakrzewska-Bielawska, 2012, p. 46).

Strategy is perceived as the orientation of an organization towards setting long-term goals and selecting programmes and plans that enable their implementation through proper allocation of resources available to the enterprise or other market entity (Ackoff, 1974; Chandler, 1962; Griffin, Singh, 1999; Harrison, 1999). Other definitions, present strategy through the prism of the way the organization is linked to its environment (Mintzberg, 1979; Stoner, 1982). The strategy of an enterprise is defined as a complex reaction process, allowing it to create and maintain satisfactory relations between the goals of the enterprise and its resources and changing conditions arising in the environment, in order to achieve the highest possible efficiency (Urbanowska-Sojkin, Banaszyk, Witczak, 2007). It should be added that not all resources determine the lasting competitive advantage of the market entity, but only those that have features defined through the prism of their value, rarity, imperfect imitability and limited substitutability (Barney, 1991, pp. 105–106). In the scientific discourse on strategy, an important place is also occupied by the ways of defining it, which emphasizes that strategy is the creation of a valuable and unique market position, and its essence is the selection of actions that will allow the enterprise to stand out from its competitors (Porter, 1996, pp. 61–78). Therefore, competitive advantage is considered a crucial element of strategy. The fact that strategy is defined as a process that allows for making decisions aimed at achieving goals completes the picture regarding the ways of defining strategy (Whittington, 1993). Despite the presence of many common elements in the definitions of strategy (goals, resources, plans, environment), the emphasis has shifted from achieving goals to the effectiveness of the organization's functioning (Dyduch, 2013, p. 14).

As a result from the analysis of the definition of strategy, approached as a long-term concept of enterprise development that specifies the goals and priority undertakings as well as the methods of achieving them, its features include a long term horizon, subordination of development activities to the set goals, and pragmatism regarding the determination of the method of strategy implementation. At the same time, it should be noted that it is difficult to clearly determine a universal time horizon of strategy for all types of organizations. However, the analysis of the literature on the subject allows for stating that the strategic perspective covers 3–5 years and more. Although the dynamics of changes in the environment are high, the time horizon determined in such a way allows for deeper changes in the organization that require going beyond the short- and medium-term scope of action. It should also be emphasized that strategy is not identified with a development plan, but with a concept, because planning is more formalized. The advantage of the strategic approach is that it makes concepts that would be excluded from the short-term perspective become real (Kaleta, 2013, pp. 41–43).

Analysis of the strategy definition indicates that in this area there is an approach in which strategy is perceived as a final product and a decision closing the process of analysing data, forecasting changes, and comparing alternative strategies. In this case, the strategy is transferred for implementation to appropriate departments, teams and organizational units. In another approach (the modern one), strategy is also treated as a long-term process, but one that never ends. Decisions are made at different stages of the process, implementation work begins, and the process of building and rebuilding the strategy is continuous (Montgomery, 2008).

Modern understanding of strategy means abandoning a one-time strategy development and then its implementation in favour of a continuous search for changes that occur inside or in the environment of the organization. Strategy in this approach becomes a bundle of options, from which the decision-maker selects the most advantageous one at a given moment. It should be added that in this case, strategic decisions are not the result of a formalized planning process but result from the actual activities of the organization (Obłój, 2007, p. 181). This means that the process of establishing a dynamic strategy should be consistent with five strategic dimensions, including scanning intensity, locus of planning, planning flexibility, planning horizon and control attributes (Barringer, Bluedorn, 1999, p. 423). As a result, this makes strategy development an interactive process, during which decisions are made in real time and there is no such thing as separating the plan from its implementation.

The multitude of ways of defining strategy is accompanied by the existence of various schools of thought about it and the development of knowledge about the practices used by managers. Among the schools of business strategy, the following schools should be indicated:

- the design school – strategy formation as a process of conception,
- the planning school – strategy formation as a formal process,
- the positioning school – strategy formation as an analytical process,
- the entrepreneurial school – strategy formation as a visionary process,
- the cognitive school – strategy formation as a mental process,
- the learning school – strategy formation as an emergent process,
- the power school – strategy formation as a process of negotiation,
- the cultural school – strategy formation as a collective process,
- the environmental school – strategy formation as a reactive process,
- the configuration school – strategy formation as a process of transformation (Mintzberg, Ahlstrand, Lampel, 2020).

The analysis of the achievements of the above-mentioned schools of business strategy shows that different trends and ways of conceptualizing it collide in thinking about strategy. In thinking about strategy, it is highlighted that strategy should be a conscious, controlled thought process, or a product of a formalized planning process, which is divided into specific stages and tasks. This is characteristic of the design school and the planning school. The positioning school in turn assumes that choosing a position on the market based on in-depth quantitative analyses is the essence of developing a strategy. On the other hand, the indication of the role of the leader, who has a vision and strategy is the distinguishing feature of the entrepreneurial school. This means that the leaders identify themselves with the strategy and promote it. The cognitive school is another school of business strategy, noticed similarly to the entrepreneurial school in management practice. It is characteristic of it that strategies appear as maps or schemes that affect the way employees perceive impulses coming from the environment. In turn, due to the complexity and variability of the organization's environment, there is also a vision of strategy as a learning process. According to the learning school, it is highlighted that the role of leaders is to manage the process of strategic learning, which consequently allows for the emergence of new strategies. The multithreaded nature of knowledge about the essence of strategy is also influenced by the fact that the context of culture and power is also considered in thinking about it. The cultural school indicates that strategies are formulated in the process of social interactions, which are based on the beliefs and values shared by the members of the organization. This is also related to the fact, as indicated by the power school, that the development of strategy is shaped by politics and power, which is found within the organization, and is revealed in the relations between the organization and entities in its environment. The environmental school indicates the role of the environment, which constitutes the balance of power for the organization and is the crucial point of the strategy. It states that the organization, reading the changes taking place in the environment, reacts to them, often focusing on clusters and market niches. At the same time, it should be noted that strategies are not developed and implemented in their pure form, i.e. in accordance with only one of the above-mentioned schools of business strategy. Therefore, the configuration school, which combines useful elements of the above-mentioned schools, contributes to the development of thinking about strategy that the process of developing a strategy can proceed in diverse ways, but it is important to adapt it to the time, context, and situational requirements.

Strategic thinking determines the creation and proper implementation of strategy. It is defined as a cognitive ability that is inherently connected with imagination, synthesis, and creativity. At the same time, it should be noted that imagination allows for combining the past, present, and future into one coherent vision (Geier, 2024, pp. 1–21). Synthesis in turn is associated with a comprehensive approach to the entire organization and resolving strategic tensions that have the nature of paradoxes, i.e. situations in which two seemingly mutually exclusive facts or adopted perspectives prove to be true at the same time. This consequently means the need to consider both the exogenous and endogenous perspectives, or to analyse the problem from the point of view of creating value for shareholders and value for stakeholders (de Wit, Meyer, 2010, p. 16).

Creativity, on the other hand, is understood as a feature that has the potential to generate creative achievements. Creativity applies to both an individual and their creative personality, as well as the team participating in the process of group problem-solving and strategy creation (Karwowski, 2009, pp. 38–41, 54–55). It should be added that creativity of a team of employees does not depend only on individual features of the employees who form the team, but also on several groups of external factors, including cultural factors. Team creativity can be strengthened by shaping a climate that is conducive to creativity. At the same time, it should be noted that it is difficult to clearly answer the question of whether a climate conducive to creativity is the cause or the effect of high employee creativity.

It is reasonable to distinguish conceptual creativity, which is necessary when developing new products, for example, from operational creativity used at the stage of selection or implementation of the effects of conceptual creativity. Increasing the creativity capital, which is the basis for the development of a creative organization, is associated with promoting such values as: the need to improve qualifications, flexibility of thinking, persistent pursuit of success, freedom in thinking and action, the ability to think holistically, the desire to break through the prevailing paradigms, openness to change, among others. These values are important from the point of view of an individual employee. However, considering the collective dimension of creativity, it is necessary to implement activities that contribute to the development of the diversity of competences, to free flow of information, as well as to increasing the responsibility and self-control of employees. Orientation to the environment is also important (Brzeziński, 2009, pp. 22–37, 67). Factors supporting the development of an organizational culture based on creativity include therefore, among others, activities consisting of promoting diversity, using the opportunities resulting from the phenomenon of open design, encouraging cooperation due to the fact that breakthrough ideas are often the result of the work of many people, involving employees of different departments and levels in the process of generating new solutions and creating situations in which there is an exchange of ideas between people representing various areas of knowledge and experience. This requires investing in infrastructure that facilitates cooperation and dedicating resources, including providing employees with time to generate innovative ideas and developing mechanisms for filtering ideas, as well as motivating employees by posing intellectual challenges. It is also important to use strategic methods or ways of thinking typical of other fields and disciplines in solving specific strategic problems, as well as using the opportunities resulting from the application of Internet technologies in stimulating employee creativity (Amabile, Khaire, 2011, pp. 116–127).

When presenting the essence of strategy and strategic thinking, it should be added that innovation is the consequence of creativity processes. In creating innovations, the key skills include associative thinking, questioning the existing status quo, observing and experimenting, as well as establishing relationships. Synthesizing based on interdisciplinary knowledge and giving new meanings to information, as well as connecting seemingly unrelated questions and problems in order to discover new ways of acting is the essence of associative thinking. In turn, questioning the existing status quo refers to formulating questions that facilitate understanding of how processes and phenomena occur and how they can be changed or improved. The purpose of observation is to draw inspiration from observing the environment, while experimenting allows for gaining new experiences and identifying cause-and-effect relationships. In the processes of creating innovations, the ability to establish contacts, expressed in creating relationships with people representing various fields of knowledge is also important (Dyer, Gregersen, Christensen, 2011, p. 12).

In general, the process of building and implementing a strategy involves having many competencies, that include integrating knowledge from different areas, critical thinking and discovering the meaning and giving meaning to what is important, unconventional thinking, but also computational thinking and drawing conclusions from large data sets, as well as managing cognitive load, and extracting useful information from noise. The role of design thinking and social intelligence as well as the ability to act in different cultural environments cannot be ignored either (Kostro, 2020, pp. 58–60).

In considerations on the essence of strategy, its connections with organizational culture, which is defined in terms of the strategic resource and autonomous nervous system of the organization (Kilmann, Saxton, Serpa, 1985), and which is created by assumptions, norms, values, patterns of behaviours shared by the members of the organization (Dessler, Turner, 1992) cannot be ignored. Organizational culture can be a source of lasting competitive advantage, and the function of the organization's bond should be indicated among the tasks it performs. The great importance attached to organizational culture in transport companies is well illustrated by the example of Southwest Airlines, where, in order to strengthen important values for the organization, a Culture Committee consisting of 120 members was established (Flamholtz, Randle 2018, pp. 8–39).

Enterprises have a better chance of achieving the goals set in their strategies if their culture and strategy are consistent with each other. However, the relationship between organizational culture and enterprise strategy can take different forms. This depends on the level of compliance of the introduced changes (in connection with shaping the strategy) with the existing culture of the enterprise and on the number of changes in the scope of key organizational factors that are necessary to implement the new strategy (Pearce, Robinson, 2014). If the implementation of the new strategy and the development of the enterprise are combined with many changes in the scope of the enterprise's functioning, and these changes are consistent with the existing organizational culture, then the enterprise is in a good position and can use the power of cultural reinforcement. Consolidating the organizational culture of the enterprise is also necessary in a situation where the implementation of the new strategy requires few changes, consistent with the current organizational culture. In such cases, it is important to communicate to employees that the introduced changes are consistent with the previous values, norms, and assumptions that co-create the organizational culture of the enterprise. The positive impact of organizational culture on the functioning of an enterprise is therefore the fact that the values, norms, and assumptions that are the basis of organizational culture provide employees with a sense of heading in one direction and, at the same time, enable individuals to identify with the enterprise. The relations between strategy and organizational culture are shaped differently if the implementation of a new strategy creates the need to introduce changes in the sphere of key organizational factors that are not consistent with the current organizational culture. In this case, achieving goals requires mitigating cultural resistance, because the currently applicable norms and values that create organizational culture have a negative impact on the enterprise and make it difficult to introduce necessary changes (Bjerke, 2004, p. 66).

When analysing the values that create the organizational cultures of transport companies, it can be stated that the following categories are often important for these companies:

- respect for diversity and ensuring a psychologically safe and inclusive environment (A.P. Moller – Maersk) (www.maersk.com/sustainability/our-esg-priorities/diversity-equity-inclusion),
- diversity and inclusion, ensuring the health and safety of all, caring for local communities, ethics, and respecting privacy as well as protecting employee and customer data (Air France-KLM) (www.airfranceklm.com/en/group/values),
- ethics and honesty, respect for human rights, sustainable development in purchasing processes (Lufthansa Group) (www.lufthansagroup.com/en/responsibility/company-and-sustainability/ethics-and-integrity.html),
- commitment to building strong communities, ethics, creating healthier environments, and developing opportunities for all (UPS) (https://about.ups.com/gb/en/our-impact.html),
- customer satisfaction and positive experience, quality, innovation, respect, care for future generations and the environment, engaged employees, innovation, and results (Stena) (https://stena.com/governance/stenas-core-values/).

These are important values both from the perspective of the expectations of external customers and employees, i.e. internal customers, as well as the challenges of modern times. The examples of the analysed transport companies confirm that the modern concept of leadership requires that leaders, while creating a better world, also consider the social interest (Mruk, 2018, p. 28). Specifically, this applies to references to sustainable development, which is a process aimed at satisfying the aspirations of the current generation in a way that allows the next generations to realize the same aspirations (Elliott, 2012, pp. 8–50). This development includes such areas as economy, society, technology, environment, and culture (Swanson, DeVereaux, 2017, pp. 78–88). It is oriented towards economic growth, equal distribution of benefits, and protection of natural resources and the environment, as well as reducing the scale of social exclusion. The essence of sustainable development is to reduce not only the scope of poverty and social exclusion but also to maintain cultural diversity. Consequently, this makes sustainable development a type of socio-economic development implemented by man and for man and integrating all human activity in the social, economic, environmental, technological, and cultural dimensions. It also represents a desirable living environment and a responsible society that implements the concept of intra- and intergenerational order (Pezzey, Toman, 2002). This is especially important in the context of the functioning of transport companies, which have many opportunities to fit into the idea of sustainable development.

1.2 The Role of Strategy as an Overarching and Long-Term Plan

The great importance of strategy for the proper functioning of an enterprise results from the fact that, together with the philosophy of operation and the operational activities conducted by the enterprise, it is one of the sources of the enterprise's success. It should be emphasized that functioning in the contemporary business environment, which is characterized by instability, complexity, unpredictability, and uncertainty, requires shaping organizational awareness and culture, strategic thinking, and flexibility in conducting operational activities. It is illustrated in Figure 1.1. It is important that there is a need for integration between organizational culture, strategy and tactical-operational activities, while maintaining the primacy of defining organizational culture, then strategy, and finally tactical-operational activities. At the same time, technological progress and development of competences mean that managers have greater knowledge resources and many

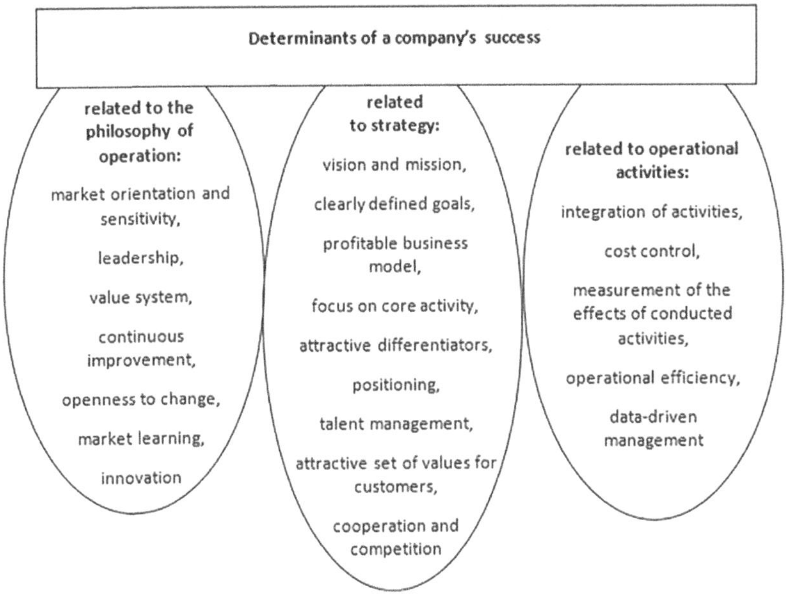

Figure 1.1 Sources of business success.

Source: Own elaboration.

tools that allow for tracking market changes and responding to them (Kozielski, 2022, pp. 45–46).

This involves shaping strategic resilience, i.e., the ability to anticipate and adapt to market trends and changes that can significantly affect the company's market situation. It allows for introducing changes before they occur in the environment (Heifetz, Grashow, Linsky, 2009).

The great importance of strategy results from the fact that the final success of an enterprise depends to a greater extent on factors related to the philosophy of operation and the strategic idea rather than on simple adaptation and efficient use of selected methods or tools. The analysis of the literature allows for stating that ineffective operational activities, with an effective strategy, provide a chance for survival, while effective operational and tactical activities with an ineffective strategy lead to failure (McDonald, Mouncey, 2009, p. 20). This also applies to transport companies.

When moving on to presenting the roles played by strategies, it should be emphasized that they depend on the approach adopted towards strategy. The analysis of the literature allows for indicating that there are various approaches to strategy, including planning-based, evolutionary, positional, and resource-based approaches. The essence of the planning approach is that creating a strategy is associated with the strong involvement of top management, attempts to predict trends, and a formalized analysis of the organization's environment and its interior, as well as a formalized process of defining goals and plans, including intermediate goals and plans. Translating strategic and intermediate goals and plans to individual units of the organization and allocating resources are also characteristic of this approach. Determining control principles aimed at recognizing the degree of goal implementation is another distinguishing feature. In turn, the evolutionary approach, assuming determinism of the environment in relation to the functioning of the organization, undermines the validity of formulating detailed guidelines as to the direction of actions. This approach emphasizes that intangible resources are the source of the organization's ability to respond to technological changes. The essence of evolutionary strategies is also the focus on creating a flexible organization, capable of adapting to changes in the environment through the use of developed methods of observation and ongoing analysis of the environment. On the other hand, the positional approach and related positional strategies focus on moving within economy sectors and searching for the most attractive areas, their selection and building a market position on them, along with its protection against competition. This approach assumes that competing is possible mainly through low costs and the possibility of reducing the price and being distinguished from competitors by providing buyers with better sets of values. The diversity of approaches to strategy is also evidenced by the fact that in the discourse on this subject, the resource approach is also important. It emphasizes that the creation of competitive advantages is made through unique resources and competences that the organization possesses or has access to (Pindelski, 2019, pp. 42–83). Consequently, this means that strategy plays many roles, which should be viewed through the prism of setting goals, identifying changes occurring in the environment and responding to them, building a competitive position, or shaping the organization's unique resources.

Emphasizing the role of strategy, the importance of which is growing in the conditions of increasing complexity of the business environment and the occurrence of abrupt changes, it should be emphasized that its basic functions include organizing development and discovering new opportunities. The organizing function means that strategy is a factor that introduces a specific order in the perception of activities conducted in the company. This is related to defining priorities and tasks of lesser importance. Organizing development is all the more important because in every company there is a need to perform various tasks simultaneously, which would consequently lead to a situation of unfavourable dispersion of resources into several initiatives. Strategic management, which is manifested in the creation and implementation of strategy, creates the possibility of assessing which of the conducted activities are the most important for the company and its market position, and which are of secondary or even tertiary significance. It should be emphasized that having a strategy and its implementation allows not only for protecting organizations from chaos and randomness of actions but also for identifying and using opportunities that would be beyond the real reach of companies, in which managers and employees would be focused on current activities. This means that the role of strategy is expressed in determining the development path and identifying new development opportunities (Kaleta, 2013, pp. 28–40).

The functions performed by strategy should also be viewed from the perspective of the fact that the right approach to it reduces the risk of strategic myopia, which is associated with failure to notice opportunities and threats, low adaptive capacity of the company, as well as narrowing the set of options considered by leaders (Czakon, 2020, p. 179).

Among the functions of strategy, its role as an integrator of elements of the internal environment (organizational structure, business units, employees, organizational culture, processes and activities, material, financial, information resources) and the external environment of the organization should also be indicated. Coordinating and combining, as well as giving direction to actions and tasks that are performed chronologically or in parallel are also the essence of strategy that indicates the usefulness of its creation. The importance of strategy is also revealed by giving it the role of a catalyst for the development of the enterprise and an initiator of changes, which can be both adaptive and anticipatory of market events, adaptive or intended, continuous and situational, planned and unplanned. However, strategy as a catalyst of change assumes that the change as such should be intended and planned and included in the enterprise's strategy (Pindelski, 2019, pp. 27, 31).

The fulfilment of functions assigned to strategy depends on whether the strategy is adapted to the environment, uses the organization's key resources, and is based on permanent differentiators, as well as on whether it is internally coherent. It is also important whether the organization has sufficient resources to implement the strategy and whether its implementation is realistic at all (Hambrick, Fredrickson, 2005, pp. 51–62).

Furthermore, it should be noted that the positive impact of strategy on the functioning of the organization can be revealed when the management makes the right decisions. In connection with this, it is important to increase awareness of the fact that the causes of making bad decisions can be various types of cognitive errors that distort the way of thinking (Kahneman, Lovallo, Sibony, 2014, p. 25) and the psychological traps associated with them, including the so-called anchoring trap, which causes people to attach disproportionately great importance to the first information received, the trap of attaching to the status quo, the sunk cost fallacy, which causes the perpetuation of past mistakes, the trap of evidence confirming one's own thesis, the trap of problem definition, the trap of overconfidence, the trap of excessive caution, or the trap resulting from attaching too much importance to critical events from the recent past (Hammond, Keeney, Raiffa, 2014, pp. 3–21).

When presenting the role of strategy as a long-term plan, the issue of dynamic technological development should be considered in the analyses, and also, a distinction should be made between infrastructure technology and corporate technology. Corporate technology, unlike infrastructure technology, is the property of a single company and has a proprietary character. Therefore, it can naturally become a source of competitive advantage. Infrastructure technologies, on the other hand, bring much greater benefits when they are used by many companies. In this case, their innovative application in the market activities conducted by companies becomes important. Consequently, this means that they can also be a source of competitive advantage. At the same time, it should be noted that at the initial stage of development, infrastructure technology can take the form of corporate technology (Carr, 2013, pp. 40–41).

The ongoing technological progress, which makes such factors as speed, omnipresence, time, and space compression of great importance, has become an important context for shaping strategy. Rapid changes mean that shaping and implementing strategy is no longer a linear process, but an interactive one, in which vision on the one hand, and financial conditions on the other hand play an important role. Within this process, fast feedback loops are of fundamental importance. They allow for understanding customer behaviour, developing propositions for them, and solving emerging difficulties in the value chain, as well as for modifying business models. The high dynamics of change means that vigilance and setting the right planning horizons are necessary. Considering the context of digital transformation, it should be noted that while doubling the company's results would be an ambitious plan achievable in the traditional world within three years, in the digital world, doubling the results achieved by the company often becomes a planning assumption for six months. This means that companies operating in the digital world need a strategy and setting strategic priorities, as well as a long-term vision, but at the same time they should update the strategy relatively often by introducing strategic initiatives, set based on observed changes that are taking place in the market and in technology. Adjusting the strategy and ways of thinking about it to the requirements of the digital world is associated with setting milestones in shorter time horizons and the need to be open to introducing changes in the sphere of methods of achieving goals (Outram, 2016, pp. 78–117).

This is even more important because digital technologies, alongside human talent, are now becoming one of the strategic resources necessary for the development of innovations, both groundbreaking and incremental. The essence of implementing new technologies is to use them in such a way that it is possible to identify the needs and expectations of consumers, leading to offering even better bundles of values (Nowicka, 2019, pp. 17–43; Westerman, Bonnet, McAfee, 2014, p. 30).

This is particularly important in the context of the functioning of transport companies, because their management is inherently connected with the implementation of new technological solutions in this area. They are used at individual stages of the value chain.

1.3 Types and Levels of Strategies

Indicating the main types of business strategies and their hierarchical nature, the following should be distinguished:

- the global strategy of the company, the formation of which is associated with the selection of areas of the company's business activity and determining those in which the organization is not interested, as well as with the acquisition of resources and their allocation between individual types of activity,
- strategies of strategic business units, which primarily consist in defining the scope of a given area of business activity and selecting the type of desired competitive advantage as well as determining the method of operation in a given industry or segment,
- functional strategies, the essence of which is related to defining how a given function (e.g. marketing, finance, research and development, human resources) is to support the achievement of the desired competitive advantage and the integration of a given function with other functions in the enterprise (Walker, Boyd, Larréché, 1999, p. 12).

This approach to strategies and their hierarchical structure is especially important in the context of transnational corporations operating in the transport industry. They are characterized primarily by their focus on knowledge, further integration, flexibility of operation, efficiency, and sovereignty. On the other hand, the structural features of these entities include, among others, dispersion and complexity in relation to the value chain and the organizational and ownership structure, as well as networking (Zorska 2007, p. 127). In addition, it should be emphasised that the activities of these companies are closely related to the implementation of the marketing approach.

In the aforementioned classification, marketing is perceived as a function. It should be noted, however, that it can be understood as a concept of the company's operations. In the latter case, it permeates the entirety of the activity, and the marketing strategy that is created on its basis also permeates the entirety of the company's activity. Considering the marketing context in the considerations about strategies and their types, it is necessary to indicate the multitude of marketing strategies. The criteria for their separation can include the company's relationship to the market and entities in the environment. Considering the company's relationship to the market, marketing strategies for entering the market, operating on the market, and exiting the market can be distinguished. In turn, the subjective structure of the environment can be a criterion for distinguishing marketing strategies towards buyers, competitors, intermediaries, and suppliers. It should be noted, however, that strategies towards competitors, suppliers and intermediaries are subordinated to marketing strategies towards buyers. The next group consists of strategies adopted in various stages of market development, product and market strategies. Strategies related to marketing instruments, including brand strategies, strategies for creating value through services, distribution and pricing strategies, as well as marketing communication strategies are also crucial (Rutkowski, 2012, pp. 20–26). It is shown in Figure 1.2.

The formulation of marketing strategies should proceed in accordance with the principles of creating a global strategy for the enterprise. This specifically applies to goals and methods of achieving them. Treating marketing strategies or other functional strategies as categories subordinated to global strategies does not mean that the relationships between them are one-way. These relationships intensify when thinking in marketing categories is present at all levels of enterprise management. However, it should be noted that in enterprises, including transport enterprises, strategy overlap which is a consequence of conflict or compatibility of strategies may occur. If the scope of strategy overlap is expanded, then the compatibility of strategies increases, but only because they are repeated at different levels of management. On the other hand, the larger the areas where the strategies do not overlap, the greater the conflicts between strategies may be observed. If such a conflict arises, it is necessary to eliminate

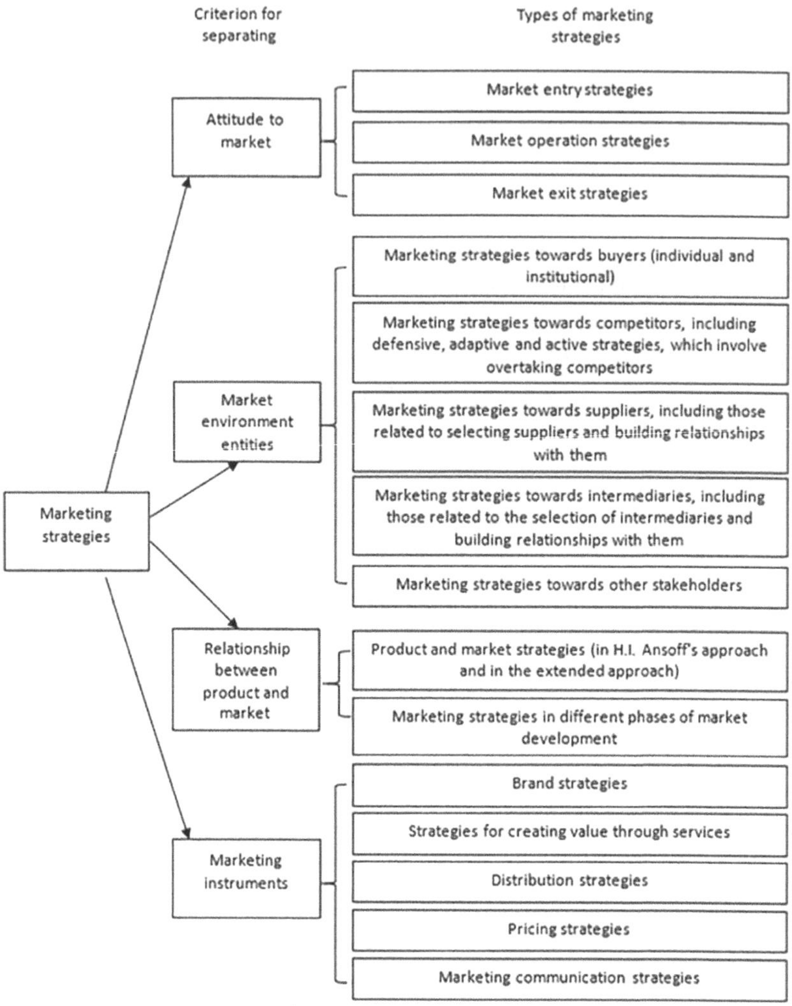

Figure 1.2 Classification of marketing strategies.

Source: Own elaboration.

the contradictions occurring between strategies. Departing from approaching marketing only as a function in favour of understanding marketing as a concept of enterprise operation may be a solution (Rutkowski, 2012, pp. 24–25).

According to another division of strategies, we can distinguish between intentional, emerging, and actually implemented strategies. It is important to note that in practice there may be situations in which an enterprise, including a transport enterprise, has all three of the above strategies at the same time. The intentional strategy expresses the intentions, priorities, and goals of the organization. If they are reflected in the activities conducted by the company, then the implemented strategy is consistent with the intentional strategy. Sometimes, however, there is a gap between an intentional strategy and the actually implemented strategy. A company may have a strategy but not implement it or, due to changes in internal or external determinants, implement a strategy that is different from what was assumed. In this case we are dealing with an emerging strategy (Czakon, 2024, p. 20).

Due to the increasing virtualization of socio-economic life, among the types of strategies, the cybersecurity strategy, the essence of which is related to the development of an innovative digital business model by designing an attractive bundle of values in the area of security, i.e. a set of benefits adequate from the perspective of customers' needs in the field of cyber protection cannot be ignored. An active approach to cyber-attacks requires the development of competences in the field of holistic business protection, and not only in the field of IT infrastructure, but also in the sphere of increasing threat awareness and proper communication with software suppliers and customers as well as other stakeholder groups. It is also important to manage the consequences of a cyber-attack and predict the potential effects of a cyber-attack on customers, suppliers, and other entities in the environment, as well as planning responses and actions to restore balance in the event of a cyber-attack. This means that in shaping key capabilities that indicate organizational resilience to cyber-attacks, it is necessary to consider the internal and external area of strategic attention and the event horizon regarding the situation before and after the cyber-attack (Hepfer, Powell, 2021, pp. 44–51).

In discussions on the strategies of transport companies, the aspect of values perceived as crucial in these companies should also be considered, as they influence the content of their strategy. Referring to the findings presented in the first point of this chapter, which concern the values important for selected transport companies, it should be noted that in the management of these companies there are strong references to the category of social responsibility, which is defined as the concept (idea) of running a company.

This responsibility results from respecting specific values by the management, employees, and company owners. It is all the more important because its absence causes chaos and contributes to destructive processes, the consequences of which are visible in the social and environmental sphere. The concept of social responsibility is reflected both at the strategic and operational level. This means that social responsibility should be recognized at the level of mission and vision, creating guidelines for defining strategic goals and guidelines for choosing the method of achieving them. However, the influence of social responsibility is noticed not only at the level of mission and vision, or goals and the selection of tools for achieving them, but also in defining the groups of the company's stakeholders and determining their needs. It is inherently connected with the types of implemented strategies. Considering the idea of social responsibility in the missions and visions of companies translates into the strategies of competition and functional strategies of the company. In the area of building competitive advantage, this means fair competition and compliance with fair play rules. At the level of functional strategies, the concept of social responsibility refers to marketing, logistics, human resources management, financial management, and sales (Stefańska, 2014, pp. 56–59).

At the same time, it should be noted that combining economic goals with social and environmental goals, which is part of the concept of corporate social responsibility, may result from genuine sensitivity and the need to do good, but may also be a consequence of the growing expectations of employees and customers, as well as other stakeholder groups of the company.

1.4 Developing, Implementing and Measuring the Effects of Strategy

A transport strategy can be shaped at the level of an individual country, a union of states, or even an enterprise conducting business activities in the transport sector. The strategies of companies providing transport services should consider not only economic and organizational issues, but also those related to infrastructure (its quantity and quality) and administrative factors related to various types of permits, concessions, and licenses for the provision of this type of services.

Various strategic solutions adopted by transport companies are influenced by the great diversity of these companies. The diversity in the functioning of transport companies is reflected in the existence of various organizational and legal forms in this area. In the transport sector, various forms of ownership also coexist, including private and public ownership. At the same time, it should be noted that the ongoing process of ownership concentration leads to a situation in which transnational corporations are playing an increasingly important role in the transport services market.

The integrated management system, which is also suitable for transport companies, includes the following stages:

- developing a strategy, which involves formulating the mission and vision (see Table 1.1) of the enterprise as well as collecting information about the enterprise's environment and its resources in the process of strategic analysis, which in turn enables the formulation and selection of a strategy,
- strategy planning, which is a detailed specification of the previous stage, which involves, among others, translating strategic goals into detailed goals concerning various aspects of the company's functioning, integrating these goals, and defining indicators to measure the degree of goal achievement, or planning the expenses necessary to implement the strategy,
- personal and organizational adaptation of the enterprise to the needs of strategy implementation, meaning adapting the organizational structure to the strategy and shaping the attitudes and behaviours of employees by informing and motivating them,
- planning of operational activities, which is inherently linked to the implementation of the strategy by creating an action plan,
- implementation, monitoring, and learning,
- testing and adaptation, which allows for assessing whether the strategic assumptions are up to date and whether the degree of strategy implementation is satisfactory, which may consequently lead to modification of the strategy or initiate the process of shaping a new strategy (Kaplan, Norton, 2010, p. 8).

Table 1.1 Examples of Mission and Vision Statements of Selected Transport Companies

NAME OF THE COMPANY	MISSION OR VISION
American Airlines	At American Airlines, our mission is to provide safe, reliable, and friendly air travel, supported by a broad range of products and services. We are committed to making each flight an enjoyable experience, prioritizing your safety, comfort, and convenience.
FedEx	FedEx Corporation will provide high-value-added logistics, transportation, and related end-to-end business services through a fully integrated digital and physical network to ultimately yield superior financial returns for its shareowners. Safety will be the first consideration in all operations. Corporate activities will be conducted to the highest ethical and professional standards. Customer requirements will be met in the highest quality manner appropriate to each market segment served. FedEx will strive to develop mutually rewarding relationships with its team members, partners, and suppliers.
A.P. Moller – Maersk	At Maersk, our vision is to transform the flow of the foods, goods, data, and materials that sustain people, businesses, and economies the world over, to enable the exchange of ideas, culture, and trust for a truly integrated world where value is created for everyone.

Source: Based on (www.aa.com/i18n/customer-service/support/customer-service-plan.jsp; https://investors.fedex.com/company-overview/mission-and-goals/default.aspx; www.maersk.com/about/vision).

There are many strategic analysis methods that can be used by transport companies. The methods of environment analysis include trend analysis, gap analysis, the Delphi method, and scenario methods, Porter's "five forces" analysis, point assessment of the sector's attractiveness, assessment of the globalization potential of the sector, map of strategic groups, or the economic profile of the sector. In turn, the methods of analysing the interior of the company include value chain analysis, analysis of key success factors, strategic balance sheet, analysis of the product and technology life cycle, portfolio methods, as well as strategic benchmarking. Among the integrated methods, which serve to analyse the company against the background of the environment, SWOT (Strengths, Weaknesses, Opportunities, Threats) analysis and strategic positioning should specifically be mentioned (Gierszewska, Romanowska, 2024, p. 9).

The choice of the target market is one of the most important decisions in the process of shaping the strategy. The purposefulness of market segmentation depends on the degree of differentiation of consumer preferences, and the more diverse these preferences are, the greater the role of segmentation (Mazurek-Łopacińska, 2021, p. 188). In the multi-stage process of making this choice, it is reasonable to consider the principles according to which the activity should be focused on such an area that gives the company the possibility of gaining a competitive advantage and to choose such a market segment or segments that are consistent with the company's strategy and ensure making profit. It is also important to focus on segments of an appropriate size and growing potential. An in-depth assessment of the barriers to entry into the market also plays an important role. The criteria for assessing the attractiveness of a market segment, which are universal and are used in many areas, including the transport industry, comprise those related to the very segment (its size, growth rate, profitability, buyers' bargaining power, homogeneity, sensitivity to the company's planned market activities, compliance with the company's strengths), as well as to competitors (their differentiation, current and entering the market, applied instruments of competition). The barriers to entry and exit from the market, the bargaining power of suppliers, or the possibility that substitutes will appear are found among the criteria related to the specificity of the market that cannot be ignored. The assessment of the attractiveness of individual market segments should also be conducted considering environmental issues and social trends, as well as political and legal conditions (Garbarski, 2023, pp. 198–200).

In the work on the strategy, various organizational solutions are adopted, because, as indicated, it is a complex process. It includes stages, among which it is necessary to indicate the strategic analysis, which serves to diagnose the conditions and potential of a given organization, the formulation of strategic goals and assumptions, making a strategic choice, within which the strategic concept of development is formulated and the implementation of the strategy, including both actions to clarify the implementation concept, as well as control and corrective actions. It should be added that although the goals can be general and specific, indirect and direct, qualitative and quantitative, it is very important to develop a method for measuring the level of their implementation. The SMART (Specific, Measurable, Assignable, Relevant, Time-related) concept is used in setting goals, according to which the goals should be specific, measurable, achievable, realistic, time-related. This is associated with assigning KPIs (Key Performance Indicators) to individual goals (Duca, 2021, pp. 452–462). They usually concern market share, sales growth dynamics, brand value, and customer capital (Kozielski, 2016). At the same time, it should be noted that the relations between the above-mentioned stages should be multilateral. It is necessary to link these stages with feedback and shape them in the form of a loop, in which the implementation of the strategy closes the entire cycle and at the same time is the starting point for the next cycle, devoted to modifying the existing development concept or creating a new one. However, introducing changes does not mean breaking with strategic continuity. Among the solutions related to work on strategy, it is worth mentioning solutions consisting in the following:

- the strategy development process is conducted by a narrow circle of decision-makers belonging to the top management, which occurs in smaller companies, but also in larger ones with charismatic leaders or in companies with extensive hierarchical structures and characterized by the presence of distance between management and employees,
- shaping the strategy is entrusted primarily to external experts, which consequently allows for the use of specialist knowledge and makes it easier to rise beyond the patterns used before in the company and above interest groups, but the problem is the lack of full access to the knowledge resources available to the company, because employees may often not want to share their knowledge with people outside the organization,
- the strategy creation process takes on a participatory nature, which is manifested by the large involvement of employees in the strategy creation phase, which translates into the fact that subsequent implementers of the strategy feel like co-creators of the strategy and identify with it; in this case, however, there may be problems with agreeing on positions, as well as problems resulting from the adoption of compromise solutions and the lack of clarity of the strategy,
- the strategy is created in specialised organizational units and teams in the company, which allows for continuous

improvement of the strategy faced with the possibilities of its implementation, but the problem in this case may be the delegation of such large competences to a relatively narrow, selected group of employees (Kaleta, 2013, p. 82, 243).

At the same time, it should be noted that the presented solutions have both advantages and disadvantages and thus are not often implemented in their pure form. This is because shaping the strategy requires developing an optimal solution based on a combination of the above-mentioned types of organizational solutions.

The process of shaping the company's strategy can be viewed through the prism of the customer engagement concept. Among the forms of customer engagement, it is worth mentioning their cooperation with the company, including the customer's participation in the development of the market offer by submitting ideas or participating in research on needs and expectations (Żyminkowska, Wiechoczek, Kieżel, Żyminkowski, 2018, p. 41).

Implementing such an approach requires both a change in the perception of the role of the customer by companies, who is no longer just a buyer but becomes a co-creator of value, or even a partner in the company (Kuusisto, Päällysaho, 2008, p. 15; Lattemann, Robra-Bissantz, 2005, pp. 194–196), as well as shaping the image of market research as a form of acquiring data, the use of which in shaping the strategy should bring benefits to both the company and the customer. This means that there is a need to develop appropriate solutions to motivate participation in market research and reduce the number of customers who would refuse to participate in it. This is even more important because the customer, by sharing knowledge, increases the intangible resources of the company (Hollebeek, Srivastava, Chen, 2019, pp. 161–185). At the same time, it should be added that the strategy implemented by the company also affects the customer's engagement.

Consequently, this means that an open approach can be used in shaping strategies, including those by transport companies. The fact that thanks to the involvement of people from outside, it is possible to benefit from obtaining solutions that would not have been created if only people from inside the company had been involved in the process is the premise for its use. Crowdsourcing solutions can be used. At the same time, it should be noted that this departure from the elitist method of creating strategies, which may also be attractive to transport companies, requires care to maintain confidentiality. It is also important that an open approach, although it can streamline all phases of creating and implementing a strategy, does not have to be used in the entire process, but only at a selected stage (Stadler, Hautz, Matzler, von den Eichen, 2023, p. 12). When considering an open approach to strategy, the dynamically developing generative artificial intelligence (AI) should also be analysed. This is illustrated in Figure 1.3.

Using the potential of generative AI in the process of creating and implementing strategies requires identifying conditions and developing effective mechanisms that allow for the synergy of human and AI, so that human abilities related to creativity, intuition, and going beyond algorithms are combined with the computational efficiency brought by AI, as well as the ability to recognize patterns and regularities based on operations conducted on large data sets. This is all the more important because the tasks assigned to generative AI, which are important from

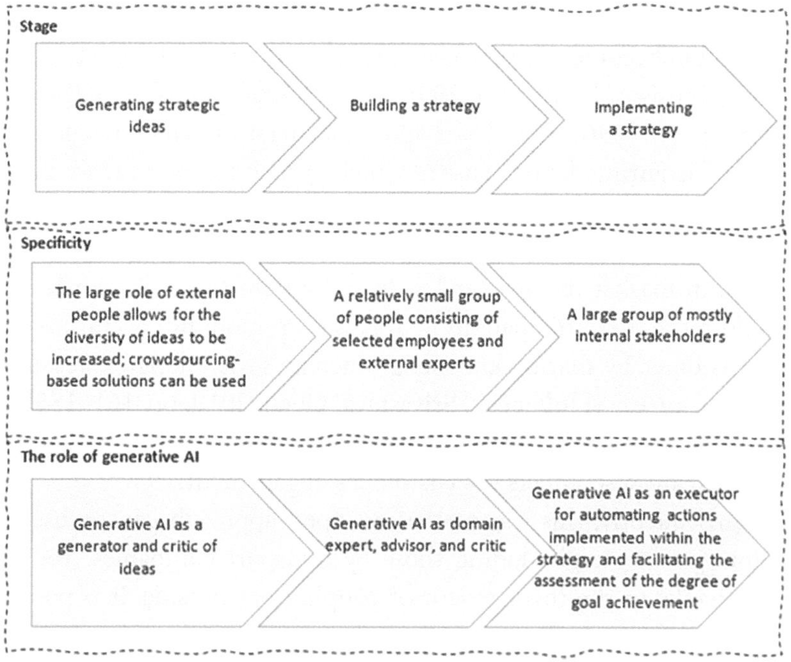

Figure 1.3 Open approach to strategy development and implementation.

Source: Own elaboration.

the point of view of its implementation in the management of market communication processes, include, among others, the role of an idea generator, a domain expert, and a critic (Przegalińska, Triantoro, 2024, pp. 18, 26–28).

The proper implementation of generative AI at individual or selected stages of strategy creation and implementation requires:

- developing competences in writing prompts,
- using search-assisted content generation that involves attaching documents to the instructions sent to the model, so that the language model can provide an answer based on the information provided,
- using instructional tuning, i.e. training the model on examples from a specified domain, which involves the need to update the model's internal parameters (Ramakrishnan, 2025, pp. 50–55).

However, before entering content into an AI model, it is necessary to check whether the person entering the materials (e.g. photos, reports containing internal company data) has the rights to these materials or appropriate authorization. This is even more important because the entered content can be used by the AI provider to train models (Michalska-Niewiadomska, 2024, pp. 104–107). This is associated with the development and dissemination of ethical standards in the use of AI. Understanding the social and ethical implications of developing generative AI, as well as their legal anchoring, proves to be important conditions for further technological progress.

Among the benefits associated with the use of generative AI, saving time and costs should also be mentioned. Generative AI can support creative thinking and support brainstorming. However, the solutions it creates are burdened with the effect of averaging and unification, as the results are often characterised by less originality. It should be noted that the machine learning process based on content generated by generative AI models can lead to the feedback effect, understood as a spiral of homogenization, in which the diversity of content created by AI gradually disappears (Castro, Gao, Martin, 2025, pp. 24–26).

Although generative AI has the potential to build knowledge about customers and market trends, as well as to create texts, music, and images, its development is accompanied by threats resulting from the emergence of deepfakes and hallucinations. These may result from contradictory or poorly formulated prompts and poor quality of data on which a given generative AI model is based, among others. The phenomenon of a single dataset cannot be ignored either, which is associated with the fact that if AI is based on erroneous, biased data, the results generated by it will also be so. Another issue is the problem of lack of transparency, which results from the fact that AI often operates on the principle of a "black box" and generates results without in-depth explanation. In addition, problems resulting from threatened privacy and data security and the lack of adaptation of solutions generated by AI to the culture of a given country, as well as from their detachment from context and linguistic nuances, are a limitation (Bostrom, 2014; Przegalińska, Jemielniak, 2023, pp. 39–40). Among the limitations of generative AI, the phenomenon known as the "curse of reversal" should also be mentioned. It results from the difficulty of language models with logical reasoning. These limitations result from the fact that the language model does not understand the question, but tries to match it to similar existing examples from the training set (Berglund, Tong, Kaufmann, Balesni, Stickland, Korbak, Evans, 2023).

It should be emphasized that the implementation of dynamically developing generative AI at selected or all stages of strategy creation and implementation should not replace the development of meta-skills among employees of transport companies, which are necessary to achieve market success. These include not only pattern recognition in large data sets, but also critical thinking, continuous learning, design thinking, and engaging storytelling instead of presenting information. The development of soft skills is also important (Dublanka, 2022, pp. 32–35).

Creating and implementing a strategy is accompanied by creative tensions. They concern both situations in which an experienced and established company enters a new market, and situations in which new companies enter established markets or new markets. Among the ways of overcoming fundamental tensions, the following issues need to be mentioned:

- moving from a fairly disciplined approach concerning opportunity selection to a flexible approach at the strategy execution stage, which should be accompanied by learning the market and adapting to unforeseen realities,

- observing, borrowing ideas, and testing them before strongly focusing on a specific business model,
- remaining sceptical about conclusions drawn from a narrow set of data and gaining knowledge from different points of view and different methods of building knowledge,
- sequentially using the wisdom of the crowd, i.e. from groups operating both inside and outside the organization,
- using heuristics to find the balance between efficiency and flexibility,
- using an attractive narrative and a coherent way of communicating the change being introduced (Bingham, McDonald, 2022, pp. 111–126).

Developing and implementing a strategy is an area where such concepts as visionary thinking, combined with imagination and risk acceptance, as well as determination and consistency in action, or pragmatism, intertwine. At the same time, it should be emphasized that there are differences between leaders and managers, because not all managers are leaders. A leader thinks primarily in the long term, and a manager in the short term. In addition, thanks to focusing on people, a leader should have the ability to make others go along with them and communicate the vision of the company's development in an attractive way and appeal to higher motivations. A leader invents, and a manager administers (Garbarski, 2021, p. 29; Koźmiński, Jemielniak, 2008, p. 36).

Developing and implementing a strategy involves making various decisions and balancing courage and correctness, vision and pragmatism, external and internal orientation, clarity and complexity, as well as variability and stability (Kaleta, 1998, p. 19–22).

At the same time, it should be added that strategic leadership is shaped based on elements, including defining the vision and general purpose of the enterprise functioning, using key competencies through the development of knowledge and intellectual capital, developing human capital and a strong organizational culture, as well as being guided by ethics and maintaining ethical practices and balancing financial control with strategic control (Ireland, Hitt, 1999, p. 47). There are also views that strategic leadership is not just a set of features and skills that leaders should have, but a complex, dynamic process that arises on the basis of interactions in organizational spaces between people and innovative ideas (Lichtenstein, Uhl-Bien, Marion, Seers, Orton, Schreiber, 2006, pp. 2–12).

Creating a strategy requires identifying technological, economic, demographic, socio-cultural, or ecological changes and recognizing the trends that provide opportunities to modify the company's operations and strongly affect changes in attitudes and buyers' behaviour on the market. It is important to formulate answers to questions about the strength of the trend's impact, which is greater the more areas of buyers' lives are subject to permanent changes under the influence of the trend. The power of the trend's impact is also determined in the context of the scope and scale of its impact, i.e. how large groups of buyers it covers. Recognizing trends requires conducting research in the context of the categories of products offered by the company and the experiences of buyers resulting from their use. Performing such research provides a basis for deciding on the selection of one of the approaches to including the trend in the organization's strategy. It includes:

- infusion of trend elements into an existing product category and expansion of the offer,
- combining trend elements and going beyond the present product category,
- counteracting the negative effects of the trend by developing products that will strengthen the value of a given product category, and the buyer will be able to avoid the effects of the development of the trend that they consider negative (Ofek, Wathieu, 2013, pp. 73–88).

The process of building a strategy is a process of negotiation character in which the opinions and views of different groups of decision-makers clash. The difficulties that emerge in shaping the strategy have their sources in operating in conditions of limited information and situations of financial and human constraints. The errors that may emerge in the process of creating and implementing the strategy include the lack of early warning systems, insufficient observation of competitors, lack of in-depth analysis of differences in strategic options and forecasting their effects, insufficient focus on creating value, insufficient connection of strategic, and operational planning, too little involvement of employees in the process of creating the strategy and insufficient control over the implementation of decisions (Cruz, Schwilling, 2004). In addition, attention should be paid to the problem of strategy becoming outdated as a result of changes in external or internal conditions (Romanowska, 2009, p. 31).

Therefore, in the process of strategy planning and its implementation, it is vital to use various data sources and apply various research methods. This requires unconventional thinking and promotes better use of the growing amount of data. Qualitative and quantitative marketing research methods are used to obtain information.

The functions of information include the exploratory function that serves to identify new phenomena and market processes, descriptive function that allows for describing these processes, and explanatory function that involves searching for and identifying cause-and-effect relationships through the use of experimentation as a research method. The functions performed by information also include reducing risk and verifying the intuition of decision-makers and, as a result, supporting decision-making processes. The innovative function of information and the competitive function (competitive advantage), as well as the structuring function that involves understanding the set goals and structuring the knowledge collected cannot be ignored either. The great importance of information in enterprise management, including a transport company, is proved by the fact that information, through its monitoring function, serves to identify risk areas early, and through its control function, to identify the effectiveness and efficiency of the conducted activities. Furthermore, information performs a prognostic function (Meffert, 2000, p. 96). Information management involves identifying the information balance between information excess and information deficiency.

It should be emphasized that it is becoming important to develop methodological solutions that allow for the proper combination of different methods and tools, as well as types of analyses, including Big Data analyses, and/or network analyses with qualitative research. The use of qualitative analysis is aimed at giving new meanings and significance to data from very large data sets. The growing importance of qualitative research results in particular from the fact that Big Data (Blok, Pedersen, 2014, pp. 1–6; Halavais, 2015, pp. 583–594;

Jemielniak, 2019, pp. 38–43) is characterized by relatively little contextualization. Conducting qualitative research should translate into a deeper interpretation and better understanding of Big Data results. This is well illustrated by the research approach consisting in triangulation of ethnographic data, which allows for contextualization and better explanation of, for example, geographical data from GPS (Hsu, 2014).

It should be emphasized that developing knowledge resources, including marketing knowledge, requires formulating answers to questions about which of the collected data are useful and what their credibility is. It is also important to determine whether all the collected data are used in decision-making processes related to shaping and implementing the strategy and whether their interpretation brings additional information or is a duplication of previous, already held information (Protasiuk, Karczmarczuk, 2018, p. 23).

In striving to develop a mechanism that would allow an enterprise to trigger a spiral of benefits generated by knowledge, it is helpful to formulate answers to the following questions:

- What added value do customer data bring in comparison to the value of the offer itself?
- How quickly does the marginal value of knowledge built on the basis of customer data decrease? How quickly does the company reach a point where additional customer data no longer leads to further improvements in the offer?
- How quickly does customer data become outdated?
- Is customer data the proprietary property of the company? Can it be acquired from another source or recreated through reverse engineering?
- How difficult is it for competitors to copy product improvements introduced based on the results of customer data analysis?
- Does data regarding a single customer help improve the product for that user or for a group of customers?
- How quickly can modifications resulting from customer data be introduced to existing products? Do modifications to the offer apply to current or future customers? (Hagiu, Wright, 2020, pp. 60–67).

The essence of managing very rapidly growing sets of data that take on a digital form is to generate solutions in which the analysis of data about one customer translates into other users of the product achieving better experiences. Data management also generates network effects when the knowledge created can be implemented quickly enough to benefit current users of the product, not just future ones. Due to the speed of transformations taking place in the environment, the role of the time factor is therefore increasing (Gregor, Kalińska-Kula, 2018, p. 166). This is consistent with the current paradigm of speed, which also applies to data acquisition, interpretation, and use in decision-making, and also requires combining the potential of human intelligence and technology.

References

Ackoff, R. (1974), *Redesigning the future*, New York: Wiley.

Amabile, T.M., Khaire, M. (2011), *Kreatywność a rola lidera*, *Harvard Business Review*, vol. 96, no. 2, 116–127.

Barney, J.B. (1991), *Firm resources and sustained competitive advantage*, *Journal of Management*, vol. 17, no. 1, 99–120.

Barringer, B.R., Bluedorn, A.C. (1999), *The relationship between corporate entrepreneurship and strategic management*, *Strategic Management Journal*, vol.20, no. 20, 421–444.

Berglund, L., Tong, M., Kaufmann, M., Balesni, M., Stickland, A.C., Korbak, T., Evans, O. (2023), *The reversal curse: LLMs trained on 'A Is B' fail to learn 'B Is A'*, *arXiv*, https://arxiv.org.

Bingham, C.B., McDonald, R.M. (2022), *Productive tensions: how every leader can tackle innovation's toughest trade-offs*, Cambridge: MIT Press.

Bjerke, B. (2004), *Kultura a style przywództwa. Zarządzanie w warunkach globalizacji*, Kraków: Oficyna Ekonomiczna.

Blok, A., Pedersen, M.A. (2014), *Complementary social science? Quali-quantitative experiments in a Big Data world*, *Big Data & Society*, vol. 17, no. 2, https://doi.org/10.1177/2053951714543908.

Bostrom, N. (2014), *Superintelligence: paths, dangers, strategies*, Oxford: Oxford University Press.

Brzeziński, M. (2009), *Organizacja kreatywna*, Warszawa: Wydawnictwo Naukowe PWN.

Carr, N.G. (2013), *IT się nie liczy. Sztuka łączenia technologii ze strategią*, *Harvard Business Review Polska*, Warszawa: ICAN Institute, 40–41.

Castro, F., Gao, J., Martin, S. (2025), *Czy GenAI zagraża naszej kreatywności?*. *MIT Sloan Management Review Polska*, no. 28, 24–26.

Chandler A.D. (1962), *Strategy and structure: Chapters in the history of the American industrial enterprise*, Cambridge: MIT Press.

Chybalski, F., Zakrzewska-Bielawska A. (2012), *Strategia i prognozowanie działalności małej i średniej firmy*, [in:] *Zarządzanie małą i średnią firmą w teorii i w ćwiczeniach*, Matejun, M. (ed.), Warszawa: Difin.

Cruz, A., Schwilling, A. (2004), *Unikanie błędów w planowaniu strategicznym*, *Zarządzanie na Świecie*, no. 1.

Czakon, W. (2020), *Krótkowzroczność strategiczna menedżerów*, Kraków: Wydawnictwo Uniwersytetu Jagiellońskiego.

Czakon W. (2024), *Jak powstają wielkie strategie? I dlaczego nie wszystkie muszą być wielkie*, Warszawa: PWE.

De Wit, B., Meyer R. (2010), *Strategy synthesis: Resolving strategy paradoxes to create competitive advantage*, Hampshire: Cengage Learning EMEA.

Dessler, G., Turner, A. (1992), *Human resource management in Canada*, Scarborough: Prentice-Hall Canada.

Dublanka, D. (2022), *Człowiek i technologia – HR przebudzenie mocy*, *Wydanie specjalne HR Personel & Zarządzanie*, no. 1, 32–35.

Duca, G. (2021), *Design of the smart objectives system in the management of a research project*, [in:] *Proceedings of the Fifteenth International Conference on Management Science and Engineering Management*, Xu, J., García Márquez, F.P., Ali Hassan, M.H., Duca, G., Hajiyev, A., Altiparmak, F. (eds.), Cham: Springer.

Dyduch, W. (2013), *Twórcza strategia organizacji*, Katowice: Wydawnictwo Uniwersytetu Ekonomicznego w Katowicach.

Dyer, J., Gregersen, H., Christensen, C.M. (2011), *The innovator's DNA: Mastering the five skills of disruptive innovators*, Boston: Harvard Business Review Press.

Elliott, J.A. (2012), *An introduction to sustainable development*, London and New York: Routledge.

Flamholtz, E.G., Randle Y. (2018), *Kultura firmy. Nowy kluczowy zasób strategiczny, którym jak najszybciej musisz zacząć zarządzać*, Warszawa: ICAN Instytut.

Garbarski, L. (2021), *Kreatywność w biznesie. Czego możemy się nauczyć od artystów?*, Warszawa: Poltext.

Garbarski, L. (2023), *Struktura strategii marketingowej*, [in:] *Marketing. Sztuka konkurowania i współpracy*, Garbarski, L., Krzyżanowska M. (eds.), Warszawa: Poltext.

Geier, M.T. (2024), *Strategic thinking: Theoretical development and assessment*, *Journal of Strategy and Management*, vol. 17, no. 1, pp. 1–21. https://doi.org/10.1108/JSMA-10-2021-0212.

Gierszewska, G., Romanowska, M. (2024), *Analiza strategiczna przedsiębiorstwa*, Warszawa: PWE.

Gregor, B., Kalińska-Kula, M. (2018), *Market Intelligence a decyzje menedżerskie we współczesnej organizacji*, [in:] *Marketing w erze technologii cyfrowych. Nowoczesne koncepcje i wyzwania*, Gregor B., Kaczorowska-Spychalska D. (eds.), Warszawa: Wydawnictwo Naukowe PWN.

Griffin, R.W., Singh, J.B. (1999), *Management*, Toronto: Houghton Mifflin.

Hagiu, A., Wright J. (2020), *Kiedy dane są źródłem przewagi konkurencyjnej, Harvard Business Review Polska*, vol. 204–205, no. 2/3, 60–67.

Halavais, A. (2015), *Bigger sociological imaginations: Framing big social data theory and methods, Journal Information, Communication & Society*, vol. 18, no. 5, 583–594. https://doi.org/10.1080/1369118X.2015.1008543.

Hambrick, D.C., Fredrickson J.W. (2005), Are you sure you have a strategy?, *Academy of Management Perspectives*, vol. 19, no. 4, 51–62. https://doi.org/10.5465/ame.2005.19417907.

Hammond, J.S., Keeney, R.L., Raiffa, H. (2014), *Myślowe pułapki, które prowadzą do złych decyzji*, [in:] *O podejmowaniu decyzji*, Warszawa: ICAN Institute.

Harrison E.F. (1999), *The managerial decision-making process*, Boston: Houghton Mifflin.

Heifetz, R.A., Grashow, A., Linsky, M. (2009), *The practice of adaptive leadership: Tools and tactics for changing your organization and the world hardcover*, Boston: Harvard Business Press.

Hepfer, M., Powell, T.C. (2021), *Uczyń cyberbezpieczeństwo strategicznym zasobem swojej firmy, MIT Sloan Management Review Polska*, no. 7, 44–51.

Hollebeek, L.D., Srivastava, R.K., Chen, T. (2019), *S-D logic–informed customer engagement: Integrative framework, revised fundamental propositions, and application to CRM, Journal of the Academy of Marketing Science*, vol. 47, no. 1, 161–185. https://doi.org/10.1007/s11747-016-0494-5.

Hsu, W.F. (2014), *Digital ethnography toward augmented empiricism: a new methodological framework, Journal of Digital Humanities*, vol. 3, no. 1.

Ireland, R.D., Hitt, M.A. (1999), *Achieving and maintaining strategic competitiveness in the 21st century: The role of strategic leadership, Academy of Management Executive*, vol. 13, no. 1, 43–57.

Jemielniak, B. (2019), *Socjologia Internetu*, Warszawa: Wydawnictwo Naukowe Scholar.

Kahneman, D., Lovallo, D., Sibony, O. (2014), *Zanim podejmiesz ważną decyzję*, [in:] *O podejmowaniu decyzji*, Warszawa: ICAN Institute.

Kaleta, A. (1998) *Cechy skutecznej strategii, Przegląd Organizacji*, no. 9, 19–22.

Kaleta, A. (2013), *Realizacja strategii*, Warszawa: PWE.

Kaplan, R.S. Norton, D.P. (2010), *Wdrażanie strategii dla osiągnięcia przewagi konkurencyjnej*, Warszawa: Wydawnictwo Naukowe PWN.

Karwowski, M. (2009), *Klimat dla kreatywności. Koncepcje, metody, badania*, Warszawa: Difin.

Kilmann, R.H., Saxton, M.J., Serpa, R. (1985), *Gaining control of the corporate culture*, Hoboken: Jossey-Bass.

Kostro, P. (2020), *Sprzedam kompetencje cyfrowe. Drogo, ICAN Management Review Polska*, vol. 4, no. 4, 58–60.

Kotler, P., Pfoertsch, W. (2008), *Zarządzanie marką w segmencie B2B*, Warszawa: Wydawnictwo Naukowe PWN.

Kozielski, R. (2016), *Wskaźniki marketingowe*, Warszawa: Wolters Kluwer.

Kozielski, R. (2022), *Rynkowy Due Diligence*, Warszawa: Wydawnictwo Naukowe PWN.

Koźmiński, A.K. Jemielniak, D. (2008), *Zarządzanie od podstaw*, Warszawa: WAIP.
Kuusisto, A., Päällysaho, S. (2008), *Customer role in service production and innovation – looking for directions for future research, Research Report 195*, Lappeenranta: Lappeenranta University of Technology.
Lattemann, Ch., Robra-Bissantz, S. (2005), *Customer integration – social and technology based concepts for a customer governance*, *Frontiers of e-Business Research*, no. 1, 193–205.
Lichtenstein, B.B., Uhl-Bien, M., Marion, R., Seers, A., Orton, J.D., Schreiber, C. (2006), *Complexity leadership theory: An interactive perspective on leading in complex adaptive systems*, *E:CO*, vol. 8, no. 4, 2–12.
Mazurek-Łopacińska, K. (2021), *Zachowania konsumentów na współczesnym rynku. Perspektywa marketingowa*, Warszawa: PWE.
McDonald, M., Mouncey, P. (2009), *Marketing accountability*, London: Kogan Page.
Meffert, H. (2000), *Marketing: Grundlagen marktorientierter Unternehmensführung. Konzepte – instrumente – praxisbeispiele*, Wiesbaden: Gabler.
Michalska-Niewiadomska, M. (2024), *Regulaminy generatywnych AI w pigułce – czyli co war-to wiedzieć, zanim skorzystamy z danego narzędzia*, *hAI Magazine*, no. 2, 104–107.
Mintzberg, H. (1979), *The structuring of organizations*, Englewood Cliffs: Prentice-Hall.
Mintzberg, H., Ahlstrand, B., Lampel, J.B. (2020), *Strategy safari: The complete guide through the wilds of strategic management*, London: Pearson.
Montgomery, C.A. (2008), *Liderzy firm muszą znów poważnie zająć się strategią*, *Harvard Business Review Polska*, vol. 65/66, no. 7/8, 60–65.
Mruk, H. (2018), *Ewolucyjny wymiar przywództwa naturalnego*, [in:] *Podejście ewolucyjne w naukach społecznych*, Polowczyk, J., Witczak, H., Błaszak, M. (eds.), Warszawa: CeDeWu.
Nowicka, K. (2019), *Biznes cyfrowy w optyce innowacji*, [in:] *Biznes cyfrowy. Perspektywa innowacji cyfrowych*, Nowicka, K. (ed.), Warszawa: Oficyna Wydawnicza SGH.
Obłój, K. (2007), *Strategia organizacji*, Warszawa: PWE.
Ofek, E., Wathieu, L. (2013), *Trendy, które mogą zmienić twój biznes. Nie przegap ich!*, [in:] *Sztuka budowania modelu biznesowego*, *Harvard Business Review Polska*, Warszawa: ICAN Institute.
Outram, C. (2016), *Digital stractics. How strategy met tactics and killed the strategic plan*, London: Palgrave Macmillan.
Pearce, J., Robinson R. (2014), *Strategic management. Planning for domestic & global competition*, New York: McGraw-Hill.
Pezzey, J.C.V., Toman, M.A. (2002), *Progress and problems in the economics of sustainability*, [in:] *International Yearbook of Environmental and Resource Economics 2002/2003*, Tietenberg, T., Folmer, H. (eds.), Cheltenham: Edward Elgar.
Pindelski, M. (2019), *Świadomość strategii i jej realizacji. Perspektywa pracowników sprzedaży*, Warszawa: Oficyna Wydawnicza SGH.

Porter, M.E. (1996), *What is strategy?*, *Harvard Business Review*, vol. 74, no. 6, 61–78.

Protasiuk, M., Karczmarczuk, A. (2018), *Strategia marketingowa*, [in:] *Data driven decisions. Jak odnaleźć się w natłoku danych*, Lutostański M.J., Galica M., Protasiuk M. (eds.), Warszawa: Wydawnictwo Naukowe PWN.

Przegalińska, A., Jemielniak, D. (2023), *Współpracująca sztuczna inteligencja w zastosowaniach biznesowych*, [in:] *Przyszłość jest dziś. Trendy kształtujące biznes, społeczeństwo i przywództwo*, Ciszewska-Mlinarič, M. (ed.), Warszawa: Akademia Leona Koźmińskiego.

Przegalińska, A., Triantoro, T. (2024), *Przenikanie umysłów. Potencjał twórczy współpracy z AI*, Warszawa: AIBooks by CampusAI.

Ramakrishnan, R. (2025), *A practical guide to gaining value from LLMs*, *MIT Sloan Management Review*, Winter, vol. 66, no. 2, 50–55.

Romanowska, M. (2009), *Planowanie strategiczne w przedsiębiorstwie*, Warszawa: PWE.

Rutkowski, I. (2012), *Istota strategii marketingowych*, [in:] *Strategie marketingowe*, Wrzosek, W. (ed.) Warszawa: PWE.

Stadler, C., Hautz, J., Matzler, K., von den Eichen, S.F. (2023), *Open strategy: Mastering disruption from outside the C-suite*, London: The MIT Press.

Stefańska M. (2014), *Rola społecznej odpowiedzialności w tworzeniu przewagi konkurencyjnej przedsiębiorstw handlu detalicznego*, Poznań: Wydawnictwo Uniwersytetu Ekonomicznego w Poznaniu.

Stoner, J.A.F. (1982), *Management*, Englewood Cliffs: Prentice Hall.

Swanson, K.K., DeVereaux, C. (2017), *A theoretical framework for sustaining culture: Culturlly sustainable entrepreneurship*, *"Annals of Tourism Research*, no. 62, 78–88. https://doi.org/10.1016/j.annals.2016.12.003.

Urbanowska-Sojkin, E., Banaszyk, P., Witczak H. (2007), *Zarządzanie strategiczne przedsiębiorstwem*, Warszawa: PWE.

Walker, O.C., Boyd, H.W., Larréché, J.-C. (1999), *Marketing strategy*, Boston: The Irwin/McGraw-Hill.

Westerman, G., Bonnet, D., McAfee, A. (2014), *Leading digital: Turning technology into business transformation*, Boston: Harvard Business Review Press.

Whittington, R. (1993), *What is strategy and does it matter?*, Boston: International Thomson Business Press.

Wojciechowski, T. (2003), *Marketing na rynku środków produkcji*, Warszawa: PWE.

Zorska A. (2007), *Korporacje transnarodowe. Przemiany, oddziaływania, wyzwania*, Warszawa: PWE.

Żyminkowska, K., Wiechoczek, J., Kieżel, M., Żyminkowski, T. (2018), *Zjawisko customer engagement wśród polskich konsumentów*, Warszawa: Wydawnictwo Naukowe PWN.

2
Intelligent Transport as an Application Area for Telematics

2.1 The Concept of Intelligent Transport and Its Importance for the Environment

The role of transport in contemporary economic and social life is perfectly reflected in the pictorial comparison which says that, if the information exchange system in the world is compared to the nervous system, then the transport system is its bloodstream (Zintegrowana Paltforma Edukacyjna Ministerstwa Edukacji Narodowej, 2025). This comparison is fully justified in the current situation, when world transport has entered the path of hyper-massification and all forecasts indicate that it will also remain on the rise in the near future. Records are being broken in the volume of container shipping from Asia to Europe, also in cargo aviation, global forwarding, and in the contract market. An upward trend is also shown by parcel handling and road transport in Europe as well as rail transport from China (Oflakowski, 2024). A significant acceleration was especially noted in the area of road transport. According to statistics, in 2015 already, the number of cars exceeded 1.1 billion, which means that there was one car for 6.5 inhabitants of the Earth. Current forecasts indicate that the number of cars will systematically increase and in 2040 it will exceed two billion (Akumulator.pl, 2025).

At the same time, the permanent increase in the number of wheeled vehicles on a global scale directly affects the increase in air pollution, especially in urban areas and causes congestion of communication routes and regional roads. Traditional cars are a source of

 DOI: 10.1201/9781003646518-3

several hundred toxic hydrocarbons, many of which have carcinogenic properties. Enormous hazard is the emission of lead, which is a systemic poison. Carcinogenic asbestos is released from car brakes and clutches, and nitrogen oxides are the main cause of photochemical smog (Instytut Rozwoju Myśli Ekologicznej, 2017). According to the *State of Global Air 2024* report, air pollution accounted for 8.1 million deaths globally in 2021, becoming the second leading risk factor for death, including for children under five years. Of the total deaths, noncommunicable diseases including heart disease, stroke, diabetes, lung cancer, and chronic obstructive pulmonary disease (COPD) account for nearly 90% of the disease burden from air pollution. In 2021, more than 700,000 deaths of children under five years were linked to air pollution; this represents 15% of all global deaths of the representatives of this age group (Health Effects Institute, 2024, p. 35).

Similarly, the development of aviation is not conducive to the health of the planet. Researchers emphasize that typical exhaust gases from aircraft engines contain four components: nitrogen (N2), oxygen (O2), carbon dioxide (CO2), as well as water vapour. Aviation fuel contains trace amounts of sulphur, heavy metals, and minerals, which, as a result of combustion, create sulphur oxides and soot and dust particles released into the environment (Kamiński, Pospolita, Cholewiński, Łagocka, 2016, pp. 487–493).

Maritime transport and inland navigation have also a negative ecological impact – on the marine environment and the cleanliness of inland waters. The problem is the discharge of ballast water from ships, greenhouse gas emissions, and oil spills. In addition, ships used in maritime transport, which sometimes escape analysis, also contribute to atmospheric pollution. As experts calculate, the power of the two-stroke main propulsion engine of some ships is even over 80 MW. Such engines, when the working process is not optimized for ecological reasons, consume from about 0.170 to 0.180 kg/kWh of ship residual fuel and emit over 0.03 kg/kWh of harmful compounds. It follows from the above that at least 24 tonnes of environmental pollutants, including sulphur oxides, nitrogen oxides, carbon monoxide, hydrocarbons, and particulate matter will be emitted into the atmosphere from such a ship within each, single hour (Witkowski, 2016, pp. 468–473).

Taking the European Union as an example, it is worth emphasizing that while greenhouse gas emissions have declined across all sectors of the economy since 1990, the trend in transport (including road transport) is the opposite. The transport industry contributes to climate change, accounting for 21% of carbon dioxide emissions in the European Union, 71% of which comes from road transport (Brzezińska, 2021). This worrying situation forces, among others, to look for technological solutions that will contribute to reduce identified threats. This is not about limiting transport in general, because its role in the economy and development of societies is a priority. Transport plays a fundamental role in the functioning of the economy, because it enables the efficient movement of raw materials, semi-finished products, and finished products between the places of their acquisition, processing, and consumption. It is also an important tool for supporting regional development – improving communication accessibility helps to activate peripheral areas, enabling their better connection with urban centres. This gives residents of smaller towns easier access to public services, education, and job markets, reducing spatial and social exclusion. It is sufficient to say that the level of a given civilization and the quality of human life is determined by the state of transport development (Wiktorowska-Jasik, 2016, pp. 15–19).

There is a need, however, to seek transport solutions that align with modern, low-emission logistics, consistent with the spirit of corporate social responsibility and the concept of sustainable development. In this context, the topic of intelligent transport systems (ITS) looks promising. Although it enables better, safer, more coordinated, and optimized use of transport networks and traffic management to minimize environmental damage, it is currently not a frequently analysed area of transport. The abbreviation ITS itself has become accepted at the first world congress in Paris in 1994 (Sussman, 2000, p. 89).

Currently, intelligent transportation programmes take many different names throughout the world; in the United States it is called ITS, in Europe – Prometheus, and in Japan it is AMTICS and RACS. They consist of technologies developed in the 1990s, such as digital maps, computers, route planning, human factors, sensors, communication, vehicle control, and traffic control, which are intended to support the development of advanced traffic management systems, travellers' information systems, vehicles' control systems, commercial vehicles' operations, systems of public transportation, and outer-urban transportation systems (García-Ortiz et al., 1995, pp. 11–81). The implementation of these solutions aims to protect the lives of road users, increase the efficiency of the transport system and protect natural resources of the environment. It also aims to provide services related to different modes of transport and traffic management which allows for better information for users and ensures safer, more coordinated, and smarter use of transport networks (Directive 2010/40/EU of the European Parliament and of the Council of 7 July 2010 on the framework for the deployment of ITS in the field of road transport and on interfaces with other modes of transport, 2010).

Genetically speaking, researchers point to three main phases of ITS technological development. In the first phase, from the 1990s to 2000, researchers focused on collecting and integrating road information and providing it to vehicles, now known as navigation technology. García-Ortiz et al. summarized technologies developed in the 1990s, pointing to Digital Maps, Computers, Path Planning, Human Factors, Sensors, Communications, Vehicle Control, and Traffic Control (García-Ortiz et al., 1995, p. 15). The second phase, from 2000 to 2010 technological paradigm was attributed to two categories. It focused on the development of cooperative driving (vehicles obtain information about the road and route through wireless communication with infrastructure and other vehicles) and autonomous driving (vehicles recognize their surroundings using cameras, radars, and sensors installed in the vehicles). In the third phase, from 2010 to the present, work is underway to combine autonomous driving with cooperative driving, involving information technology and IT companies. The vehicles are intended to, de facto, drive themselves. Route calculations and corrections are performed using a range of technologies, such as satellite navigation, sensors, big data, and algorithms. As examples, the researchers cite Google's autonomous car, which began road testing in 2009, and later autonomous driving systems such as Apple Car, BMW's Personal Pilot Pro system, Toyota's Teammate Advanced Drive system and Tesla's Full Self-Drive system (Duan, 2023, pp. 1–17).

There are many definitions of ITS, but in the general sense they are systems using various technologies – information technology, telecommunications, and automation in the field of transport – ITS combine telecommunications, electronics, and information technology with transport engineering to plan, design, operate, maintain, and manage transport systems (Directive 2010/40/EU of the European Parliament and of the Council of 7 July 2010 on the framework for the deployment of ITS in the field of road transport and on interfaces with other modes of transport, 2010). First of all, they cover infrastructure (see section 2.3), vehicles, and their users (see section 2.4) serving for traffic and mobility management. They use advanced methods of traffic management for car, rail, public transport, for airplanes and ships; systems supporting fleet management and cargo transport; advanced vehicle driving assistance systems; automatic toll collection systems; automatic control of compliance with regulations; dynamic systems of users' informing (Marczak, 2014, pp. 34–42). Intelligent transportation systems (ITS) combine therefore information technology, vehicle electronics and mobile telecommunications, which allows for better planning, servicing, design, maintenance, and management of transport. Intelligent systems based on telematics are a tool that find a use in all branches of transport (Koźlak, 2018, p. 5). They are not only used in road transport, but they are also being developed in water, rail and air transport (see section 1.2); however, the predominant scope of ITS functionality is dedicated to road transport, what means in practice that these systems are mainly used in this branch of transport.

Directive 2010/40/EU of the European Parliament and of the Council of 7 July 2010 on the framework for the deployment of ITS in the field of road transport and on interfaces with other modes of transport states that ITS are advanced applications which – although they are only information carriers in themselves – are intended to provide innovative services related to different modes of transport and traffic management, and allow for better information for different users and ensure safer, more coordinated, and smarter use of transport networks (point 3). The European Union is committed to promote usage of information and communication technologies in the road transport sector and its interfaces with other modes of transport, as such technologies can significantly enhance the environmental performance, efficiency (including energy efficiency), safety and security of road transport – particularly the transport of dangerous goods – as well as public safety and the mobility of passengers and goods. This commitment also supports the proper functioning of the internal market and contributes to increased competitiveness and employment. However, the deployment of ITS applications should not prejudice national security interests or measures necessary for defence purposes (point 4) (Directive 2010/40/EU of the European Parliament and of the Council of 7 July 2010 on the framework for the deployment of ITS in the field of road transport and on interfaces with other modes of transport, 2010).

The above-mentioned directive is binding but not normative, which means that the choice of means by which the intended goal is to be achieved remains within the competence of individual countries. However, according to researchers, ITS always consist of three parts, in particular (Mazurek, 2010, p. 1):

- executive one (e.g. signs with various content, traffic lights),
- measuring (various types of road sensors),
- algorithms of control (Długosz et al., 2021, pp. 42–47).

ITS utilize many existing systems and technologies. These include:

- Satellite navigation systems, such as GPS, which enable determination of precise location of vehicles and users, as well as planning optimal travel routes,
- Systems of dynamic traffic lighting that adapt traffic signals to traffic volume and minimize delays,
- Road traffic monitoring systems using cameras, sensors, and detectors that enable traffic flow analysis, road incident detection, and driver behaviour monitoring,
- Passenger information systems, such as information boards at stops, mobile applications or audio systems which provide passengers with information on timetables, delays or, e.g. route changes,
- Vehicle-to-vehicle (V2V) and vehicle-to-infrastructure (V2I) communication systems that enable the exchange of information between vehicles and infrastructure to warn drivers of road hazards,

- Vehicle monitoring systems using GPS, sensors and communication systems that enable monitoring of vehicle location, its technical condition and driver behaviour (Encyklopedia zarzadzania, 2025).

Passenger cars are also changing in terms of ITS because, as research shows, they are the most popular and widely used means of transport (Jędrzejczyk, 2024, pp. 5205–5213). The already quite common automatic collision warning systems and automatic emergency braking systems contribute to improving safety. Also, special sensors installed in cars ensure their proper functioning in terms of safety, fuel consumption, maintaining the appropriate fuel mixture composition and regulating the engine speed. Important functions are performed by the following:

- a set of ESP system's sensors (of wheel rotational speed, vehicle speed, torque, lateral acceleration, gearbox) which stabilize the driving track in the situation of potential skidding;
- Lambda sensor, which measures oxygen levels in the exhaust system and allows for fuel injection modifications. Data from the sensor are transmitted to the computer on a bipolar basis (lean/rich mixture),
- the boost pressure sensor (of turbine) controls the amount of air supplied to the engine and influences the regulation of the fuel-air mixture composition;
- crankshaft and camshaft position sensors affect how the engine performs and whether the car meets exhaust emission standards;
- coolant temperature sensors in the car, which support the regulation of the fuel mixture composition;
- Manifold Absolute Pressure (MAP) sensor, which informs about engine operational working.

The use of ITS tools, including the previously mentioned traffic monitoring cameras, traffic density sensors, dynamic traffic light systems, GPS, etc., improves the flow of ecological and safe vehicles on the roads, eliminates delays, and leads to reduction in fuel consumption, which de facto changes the current approach to road traffic management. For example, thanks to sensors placed on the road, it is possible to constantly monitor traffic intensity on individual road sections and, based on this information, adjust traffic lights as needed. This allows for minimalization of delays and creation of smooth traffic flow, which contributes to shorter travel time and reduced emissions. For example, lane control (their opening and closing), which is particularly important during rush hour is also possible. Based on data analysis, the manager can also allocate more lanes for traffic in one direction, which helps to reduce traffic congestion by accelerating the flow of vehicles.

Traffic information systems, in turn, provide drivers with information about disruptions, accidents, and detours (variable message signs – see Figure 2.1). The ability to receive such information in real time allows for faster route adjustments and to avoid high-traffic areas (Encyklopedia zarzadzania, 2025).

ITS are also crucial for public transport. For example, a passenger information system is being developed, including special information boards at stops, mobile applications, and audio systems. This system allows passengers to be informed about disruptions, such as delays and route changes, and to track up-to-date timetables. This information is provided on an ongoing basis and can be tracked by passengers in real

Figure 2.1 Variable message signs – Drivers' information system.

Source: Official website of General Directorate for National Roads and Motorways: www.gov.pl/web/gddkia/znaki-zmiennej-tresci---tak-samo-wazne-jak-tradycyjne.

time. In addition, ITS is used to monitor passenger behaviour, detect, and quickly respond to incidents, disturbances in order, or crimes, which makes traveling by public transport much safer.

Another comprehensive component of ITS is the fleet management system, made possible by equipping vehicles with GPS and sensors. The fleet management system is an advanced IT tool that enables comprehensive monitoring, coordination, and optimization of the operation of vehicles belonging to a single transport operator. This is a major achievement, considering that thanks to the ongoing acquisition of data on the speed, position, technical condition, and fuel consumption of vehicles, it is possible not only to effectively plan routes and manage drivers' working time, but also to quickly respond to unforeseen situations and difficulties such as breakdowns, traffic jams, or road accidents. These systems also allow for the collection of real-time information on traffic conditions, which translates into improved transport flow and increased safety. Additionally, when transporting goods requiring special conditions, such as food or medicine, it is possible to continuously monitor the temperature and humidity inside the cargo space, significantly improving the quality of transport services. As a result, fleet management systems are becoming an indispensable element of modern logistics and road transport, contributing to increased operational efficiency and reduced costs as well as environmental impact.

In summary, the concept of ITS brings a range of benefits of a diverse nature, contributing both to improve the quality of life for people and to environmental protection. As this study attempts to demonstrate, these benefits are primarily economic in nature, manifesting themselves in increased efficiency of transport processes, optimizing road traffic management, and reducing operating costs related to infrastructure and vehicle operation. The use of ITS also helps to reduce losses resulting from delays, accidents, and inefficient use of resources.

No less important are the ecological benefits resulting from the reduction of greenhouse gas emissions, other air pollutants, noise, and energy consumption. By improving road traffic and promoting alternative, more ecological forms of transport, such as public transport or cycling, these systems play an important role in shaping sustainable urban mobility. Social benefits, in turn, include increased safety of road users, improved access to transport services, especially for people with communication disabilities as well as increased comfort and predictability of travel.

ITS also contribute to improving the quality of public transport services through better route planning, real-time traffic monitoring, providing passenger information, and faster responding to emergency situations. Moreover, one of the key aspects of their implementation is increasing safety – both in the context of preventing road accidents and protecting transported people as well as cargo, including dangerous goods. As a result, ITS constitute an important element of sustainable development policy, enabling the creation of more functional, safe, and ecological transport systems that respond to the challenges of modern society and its transportation needs.

2.2 Branches and Types of Transport

Since the dawn of time, people have sought to meet their transportation needs, which result from the different distribution of people around the world, and the non-identical location of resources necessary for their survival and functioning. There are many sources of transportation needs. Centuries ago, people began to move in order to meet basic physiological needs (food, shelter), but today they are also guided by other goals, including political, military, trade, development of knowledge, as well as social and cultural ones (Andrzejewska et al., 2013, p. 1029). Advanced technological solutions that aim to increase the efficiency, safety, and sustainability of transport in accordance with the concept of sustainable development are ITS. Importantly, they are not limited to one form of movement only, but cover various modes of transport, integrating them within one, coherent information infrastructure. This enables smooth traffic management, travel time optimization, better logistics planning, and rapid response to emergency situations, as described in the previous subchapter.

The development of ITS allows for the creation of smart regions and cities, in which individual means of transport cooperate with each other, creating the so-called: intermodal systems. This means that, for example: a train, bus and a rented public bike can be coordinated in such a way that the entire travel process is as smooth, economic and ecological as possible. These technologies support both individual passengers and the freight transport sector, increasing the competitiveness of the economy and the comfort of life of residents. Researchers emphasize that ITS are not about technology for its own sake – they are about using technology to make transport safer, cheaper, cleaner and more efficient, across all modes (Demeyer et al., 2014, pp. 112–123). In other words, the idea of ITS is not the technology itself, but its practical application in all forms (branches and modes) of transport, so that it serves people, the environment and the economy. In the face of the growing challenges of urbanization, climate change and mobility, ITS are becoming the foundation of modern and sustainable communication systems.

ITS cover all major branches of transport, as mentioned above, integrating them to improve the efficiency, safety, and sustainability of mobility. Transport operations are carried out in various environments – land, water, and air (Długosz, Zimniewicz, 2009b, p. 164). Therefore, three basic types of transport, named after these environments can be distinguished (Żak, 2009, p. 142). In each environment, different means of transport are used to move people and goods (Kacperczyk, 2009, p. 7). The diversity of the principal means of transport used in the three environments provides the basis for distinguishing between the branches. Researchers typically list the principal ones as follows:

- car transport: It is sometimes colloquially referred to as road transport. Although such terminology is commonly used, from the point of view of linguistic precision and transport classification, it is a simplification or even an error. The nomenclature road transport suggests that it is the road as an element of infrastructure that is the basis for the classification of a given transport branch. Meanwhile, roads – understood more broadly as designated traffic routes – also occur in other transport branches, such as tracks in rail transport, water shipping routes or air routes in aviation. Therefore, using the term road exclusively for car transport does not fully reflect the infrastructural reality of other branches, which also operate within strictly designated and organized routes of movement. Anyway, this type of transport is currently considered the most developed area of ITS applications. It includes, among others, intelligent traffic management, traffic monitoring systems, traffic light signals dependent on traffic intensity, real-time information for drivers using electronic variable message signs (VMS), electronic toll collection systems as well as solutions supporting safety, such as accident detection and incident management systems.

- Rail transport is based on the movement of goods or passengers using trains running on rails (Urbanyi-Popiołek, 2013, p. 11). A train is a combination of wagons or other railway vehicles in the appropriate order so that they can be pulled by at least one locomotive or have an independent drive. Today, non-passenger transport carried out by rail is dominated by bulk cargo. Traditional goods such as coal, iron ore, grain, fertilizers, steel products, construction materials, and petroleum products predominate here. They constitute over 90% of all cargo handled by rail transport (Neider, 2015, p. 75).
- Shipping, which encompasses all types of water transport, including all inland and maritime carriage. It is an age-old form of human activity. Even today, in the era of globalization and environmental protection, this type of transport plays a crucial role. In addition to transporting people, it allows for the unlimited transportation of various goods over vast distances, in various forms and at the lowest possible cost. Maritime navigation is present in virtually all waters around the world (including oceans, seas, natural connections between them, artificial seaways, enclosed seas, and sea-river canals). It is effective and popular mainly in intercontinental transport, while in inland waterway transport, shipping depends on infrastructure – primarily the presence of ports and the layout and length of inland waterways (Wyraz, 2016, p. 714).
- Air (plane): The first airplane was constructed not a long time ago (just over 100 years), but the most daring interpretations of the beginnings of aviation date back to the 16th century. In 1505, already, Leonardo da Vinci formulated the principles of flight in the Bird Flight Code (Kowalska et al., 2023, p. 108). Nowadays, air transport has become one of the most important branches of transport, playing a significant role in the global

communication and logistics systems. First of all, it offers the possibility of moving people and goods from very distant places in the world, in a relatively short time, which is particularly important in the context of the increasing pace of life and the dynamically developing world economy. Thanks to this, it is used wherever delivery time is a priority factor – for example, in the transport of high-value goods, medical materials, or spare parts for devices requiring immediate repair. In this branch, however, the costs associated with quick service definitely play a large role. They are much higher than in the case of land or water transport of goods (Scheibler, Puchała, 2021, p. 106). Aviation, compared to land or sea transport, generates much higher expenses related to fleet operation, maintenance of airport infrastructure, logistic security, and technical service.

- Transmission transport is a type of transport in which goods are moved using pipelines, cables, or other transmission installations. This branch will not be considered more broadly in the context of ITS because, although it is an effective method of transport that minimizes operating costs and environmental impact, it is also very specific and separate from other branches. It is mainly used to transport electricity and liquid, gas, and bulk raw materials, such as crude oil, natural gas, water, and so on (Kautsch, 2018, p. 8).

The infrastructure of each specific transport branch is composed of so-called linear and point elements (subsection 2.3). They are needed to transport people and to realize deliveries of goods using various means of transport. When choosing them, speed, frequency, reliability, access, and cost are taken into account (Rabe, 2019, p. 82). In turn, the means of transport of the individual branches are used individually or together to implement different types of transport (see Table 2.1). Experiences reveal that each branch of transport and different types of transport are interrelated and complementary to each other.

A specific type of transport that utilizes means of transport from different branches (hence its name) within a single transport route – such as rail, trucks, and ships – is inter-branch transport: intermodal, multimodal, and combined. For many years, these terms were defined ambiguously. In both the academic literature and documents of the

Table 2.1 Types of Transport in Modern Intelligent Transportation Systems

TYPE OF TRANSPORT	CRITERION OF DISTINCTION	CHARACTERISTICS
Passenger and freight	Subject of transport	Transport is an inseparable element of the functioning of both individuals and the entire society. Without it, it is impossible to get anywhere or deliver necessary goods. In the first case, we are talking about passenger transport, which enables the daily movement of people – to work, school, offices, or places of rest. In turn, freight transport plays a key role in the functioning of the economy. It is thanks to it, that it is possible to efficiently move goods, raw materials, and products – both at the local and international level.
Regular and irregular	Method of transport's organization	The method of organizing transport divides it into two groups: regular one, including planned and repeated journeys (e.g. in public transport) and irregular, which may include charter or occasional transport.
Private and public	Form of ownership of the means of transport	Public transport, unlike private transport, is available to everyone, runs at set time intervals, and on specific routes. Its existence and operation are a response of public institutions to the transport needs of all members of the community. It reflects the authorities' desire to provide citizens with access to communication services and is implemented using means of transport that do not belong to private individuals.
Domestic and international	Territorial scope	This criterion allows one to distinguish between domestic transport, which takes place within the borders of one country and international transport, which includes transport between countries.
Groupage and full truckload transport	Cargo space occupancy	Full truckload transport is a form of transport in which the entire cargo space of a vehicle is reserved for one customer. Regardless of whether their load fills the entire space or not, the customer pays for the full vehicle capacity. This usually results in direct delivery from the shipper to the recipient, without reloading. This is different from groupage transport, where the cargo space is shared among multiple shippers (each customer pays only for the part of the space used and must take into account the need to reload at a certain stage of the journey).

Sources: Own elaboration based on Kautsch (2018) and Konieczna (2024).

European Commission, as well as in practice, they were often used interchangeably (Czermański, 2011, p. 48). Multimodal transport means carriage of cargo between the point of origin and the point of destination using at least two modes of transport, based on one transportation document. Its narrowing is intermodal transport, which means transporting cargo in the same loading unit (e.g. container, swap body, semi-trailer) based on a single transport document and using different modes of transport, but without reloading the goods themselves along the entire transport route. Only the loading unit is transferred (Brill, Łukasik, 2024, p. 12). In intermodal transport, extensive usage of containers, railcars, self-unloading platforms, self-unloading wagons, and intermodal ferries is made, which are closely synchronized, allowing for a smooth transition between them. Combined transport can be considered as one of the types of intermodal transport, which should be understood as transport in which a loading unit is transported in long-distance traffic by rail or ship, while its delivery and removal is carried out by road over the shortest possible distances.

The essence of a multimodal transport system is therefore to use the specific features and advantages of individual modes of transport in a single transport process. This involves integrating more flexible road transport (faster and cheaper for short distances) with cheaper and faster for medium and longer distances due to greater load capacity as well as more reliable and environmentally friendly rail, sea, or inland waterway transport in the entire transport chain. This type of transport is currently gaining popularity, especially in international trade. Its main advantages are lower transport costs over long distances, less environmental pollution, and greater logistic efficiency. Its popularity in Europe is also growing thanks to support from the European Union, focused on sustainable development and due to the expansion of terminal infrastructure.

2.3 Characteristics of the Infrastructure Enabling Movement

The infrastructure of each transport branch is made up of linear and point elements, the presence and proper technical condition of which are a necessary condition for the proper course of transport processes

(Mendyk, 2009, pp. 170–172). In some studies, the authors limit themselves to a simplified approach, according to which linear transport infrastructure is a system that includes roads and railways (European Conference of Ministers of Transport, 2004, p. 223). In a more developed approach, it means roads and natural and artificial routes where means of transport and often directly materials and products, move (Ficoń, 2009, p. 60). It is therefore assumed that these are man-made, permanently located basic road facilities (Wojewódzka – Król, 2007, p. 104), or to put it another way, the existing network in the country understood as any separated strip of land intended for the movement or parking of means of transport, together with the engineering structures located within it (Fertsch, 2006, p. 64). In the above sense, linear transport infrastructure should include not only roads of all modes of transport, but also various types of auxiliary equipment used directly to service these roads (Ciesielski, 2006, p. 107). It should be emphasized that the roads of some branches are artificial, while others have natural character (Figure 2.2).

Artificial roads are man-made. Those are transportation routes entirely designed and constructed by humans, using appropriate engineering technologies, and materials. Examples of this type of infrastructure include highways and railways. All of them require significant financial outlays both at the construction stage and for subsequent maintenance. In contrast, natural roads were created without significant human intervention and their adaptation for transport purposes is usually limited to designate course of the route and to possible minor

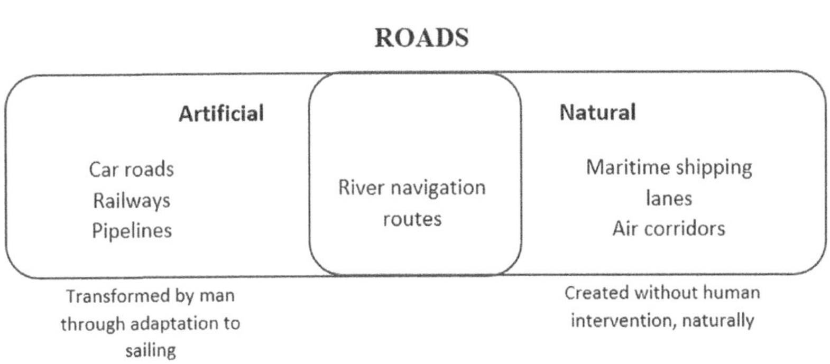

Figure 2.2 Distinction between artificial and natural roads.

Source: Own elaboration based on Neider (2006).

cleaning works or marking. Therefore, the use of natural routes for transport does not involve the necessity of incurring costs related to their construction and operation (Nowosielski, 2008, p. 153). Natural routes are primarily air corridors, natural mountain passes historically used as trade routes or sea routes, but, as researchers emphasize, in maritime transport we also deal with typical elements of artificial routes. These are primarily canals, such as the Suez or Cologne canals, whose characteristic feature is that they were entirely designed and built by man in order to create a navigable waterway where natural conditions did not allow for it or were insufficient. The construction of the canal requires earthworks, engineering works, and the use of appropriate hydrotechnical infrastructure, such as locks, embankments, and dams (Neider, 2006, pp. 23–24).

When it comes to rivers, they exhibit characteristics of both natural and artificial pathways (Figure 2.2). This is due, among other things, to the need for human preparation for navigation purposes through activities such as canalization, regulation, and deepening. It should be emphasized that the inland waterway network, in addition to river routes that are difficult to clearly classify, also includes elements of a typically artificial nature. These include, as in the case of maritime transport, shipping canals, and retention reservoirs (Wojewódzka-Król, 2008, p. 98).

The linear car transport infrastructure constitutes the existing car road network, understood as a network of structures together with road engineering structures devices and installations, constituting a technical and operational whole intended for car road traffic management, located in the road lane. According to the legislation of most countries, it is the land demarcated by boundary lines, together with the space above and below its surface, in which the road, construction facilities and technical devices related to the management, security, and service of traffic are located, as well as devices related to the needs of road management (Kancelaria Sejmu, 2007, p. 2). It should be emphasized that in each legislation, two basic types of car transport routes are usually distinguished (Grzybowska, 2009, p. 196):

- Public, i.e. those that can be used by anyone in accordance with their intended purpose, with restrictions and exceptions specified in the relevant regulations. They are owned and managed by the relevant state administration bodies. Further, public roads can be divided according to various criteria, e.g. their importance in the road network or the degree of accessibility and service of the adjacent area (motorways, expressways, publicly accessible).

- Internal, i.e. roads which are not classified into any category of public roads. These are usually roads running through housing estates, retail parks, access roads to forest, and agricultural land, to facilities used by businesses, squares in front of railway stations, etc. They may be publicly accessible (e.g. an access road to a supermarket) or not publicly accessible, e.g. roads in gated communities.

Various types of engineering structures, devices, and installations are located along each type of above-mentioned roads. Engineering structures included in the linear car transport infrastructure include bridge objects (bridges, viaducts, overpasses, footbridges), various types of tunnels, culverts (for watercourses, animals, technical devices), and retaining structures (structures designed to maintain the stability of an embankment or excavation). Whereas technical devices for directing and securing traffic on roads include road signs, traffic lights, soundproof screens, snow fences, dividing fences, protective nets, etc. In addition, along roads of car transport, there may be facilities such as parking lots, bays, sidewalks, bicycle paths, exits, parking areas, etc.

The linear infrastructure of rail transport consists of railways, together with a designated strip of land and the engineering structures located along them, as well as traffic control devices (TCD) and data transmission devices, i.e. communication ones (Wojciechowski et al., 2009, pp. 231–239). The latter provide information on train movement and other data related to passenger and freight service. Engineering structures found on the railway line include bridges, viaducts, tunnels, platforms, elevated passages, underground passages, buildings (e.g. at guarded railway crossings). On the other hand, railway TCDs are designed to ensure traffic safety and efficiency. They enable the control of track and turnout occupation, the control of train speed and braking, and also make permission to run dependent on the position of the switches. One of the basic types of TCD devices is trackside signalling equipment, designed to transmit signals related to train movement or shunting. The others include (Towpik, 2009, p. 61):

- setting devices for positioning switches and signals,
- devices that supply electricity to individual TCD devices' elements,
- connecting devices that integrate individual TCD devices' components into entire whole,
- closing, interlocking and control devices, the task of which is to close the devices that are part of the route in the appropriate position and to implement the interdependencies between the individual elements of the route and individual routes in order to safely and efficiently conduct railway traffic; in addition, these devices perform the function of monitoring the status of individual elements that are components of the setting and signalling devices.

A railway road is also called a railway line (Zalewski, Siedlecki, Drewnowski, 2004, p. 23). It is made up of two main elements (Figure 2.3). The first is the roadbed, which must have adequate resistance to various types of deformation because it is responsible for absorbing the loads from the rolling stock. The railway superstructure is constructed on it (Figure 2.4), the basic component of which are the rails. The cross-sectional shape of a rail is similar to that of an I-beam (the rail is primarily subjected to bending). It consists of three

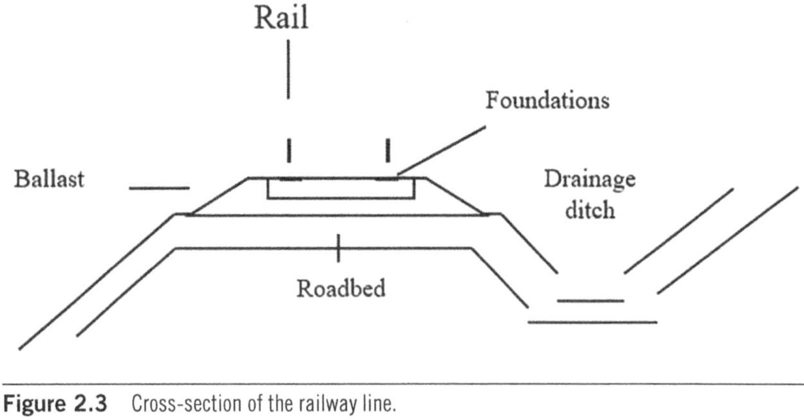

Figure 2.3 Cross-section of the railway line.

Source: Own elaboration based on Sysak (1982).

Figure 2.4 Standard (traditional) railway track.

Source: Author.

parts: the head (the upper part of the rail, designed to accommodate rolling stock wheels and direct their travel), the foot (the lower part, designed to be attached to the pad and sleeper), and the neck (the intermediate part between the head and foot).

It should be added that in many countries, e.g. in Poland, Austria, Germany, Great Britain, the Czech Republic, Qatar, and Australia, a new type of ballastless surface is being tested (Figures 2.5 and 2.6), which is characterized by high durability and stability, as well as limited vibration and noise during train passage (Portal Kolejowy, 2025). This is due, in part, to social pressure to make usage of modern and quiet solutions. Until now, ballastless surfaces have been used primarily on bridges and viaducts (Kraśkiewicz, Oleksiewicz, Lipko, 2016, pp. 101–114). They typically consist of continuously welded steel rails mounted on prestressed concrete sleepers, which are placed on a stable ballast bed or, increasingly, on ballastless slab track systems.

Figure 2.5 Example of a ballastless surface (grass technology, also known as green technology).

Source: Transportszynowy.pl: www.transportszynowy.pl/Tramwaje/torytrambezpodsypka.

Such solutions reduce vibration, noise, and maintenance needs, while allowing higher speeds and heavier loads. Advanced materials, elastic pads, and under-sleeper mats are also used to extend track life and improve ride comfort.

Technological progress and increased competition have continued, primarily in the market for crossing surface systems. Road-rail crossings are now equipped with ballastless surfaces or surfaces made of synthetic materials (e.g. rubber), often recycled. Currently, widely used road surfaces at railway and road crossings can be divided into five groups (Dąbrowski, Stencel, 2016, pp. 47–68):

1) ballastless surfaces,
2) rubber slab surfaces,
3) small-sized slab surfaces,
4) large-sized slab surfaces,
5) wooden beam surfaces (drylines).

At this point, it is also important to note the innovative potential of combining traditional rail systems with the vision of future ultra-fast solutions, such as hyperloop. For example, MagRail tests confirmed that rail vehicles can operate seamlessly on existing frictionless rail tracks, meaning they can travel over them rather than on them (Nakolei.pl website, 2023).

Railway lines can be differentiated according to various criteria. One of the most common is the division according to technical and operational parameters. The basis for such a division is the speed of passenger and freight trains, traffic intensity, and curves' radii. In order for a line to be classified in a specific category, it must meet established qualification criteria. The distinction between the routes on which trains move can also be made by taking into account factors such as the number of tracks, their width, the type of traction used, the shape of terrain, the position of the line in relation to the ground surface, or the type of control devices being used.

Moving on to discuss linear infrastructure used in maritime transport processes, it is important to emphasize that it consists of both

Figure 2.6 Example of a ballastless surface (prefabricated slab technology with continuous rail support KC/ERS).

Source: Transportszynowy.pl: www.transportszynowy.pl/Tramwaje/torytrambezpodsypka.

natural and artificial waterways. Sea and ocean shipping routes (to and from ports) constitute natural linear infrastructure, while canals, intended to shorten maritime navigation times, are, as already mentioned, artificial in nature. Some authors (Wojciechowski et al., 2009, p. 246), (Basiewicz et al., 2007, p. 144) to the linear infrastructure of maritime transport also include fairways in port aquatic areas (in port aquatories area – the water part of the port – ships manoeuvre and stop for maintenance purposes). The outer part of the aquatorium is the roadstead, i.e. the place where vessels are waiting before entering the port (Gołembska, Szymczak, 2004, p. 80; Gołembska, 2009, p. 95). Other researchers disagree, they do not consider them as a component of linear infrastructure. They justify this by arguing that aquatoriums constitute an integral part of ports. Therefore, the tracks located within them should be categorized as part of ports which are, in turn, the most important elements of point infrastructure.

Natural shipping routes run through the entire ocean, which includes, among others: open oceans, coastal, and inland seas, natural connections between seas and oceans (straits and natural canals), enclosed seas and sea-river canals. Theoretically speaking ships can move freely across the ocean, and traffic restrictions occur only in channels, in straits and port approach areas, where strictly defined traffic rules apply and ship captains must strictly adhere to them (Neider, 2006, p. 31). On the other hand, however, the captain is almost always obliged to sail along a route that is safe from the point of view of navigation and will take him to the destination port as quickly as possible. In practice, this means that ship routes usually coincide with mileage of proven routes, determined on the basis of many years of navigation experience.

The artificial element of the linear maritime navigation infrastructure are man-made sea canals. Their construction and maintenance require large financial outlays, and often also innovative solutions in the field of technical thought, which must take into account the natural conditions in which they are located. The three most important artificial navigation routes are considered to be the Suez Canal, the Panama Canal, and the Cologne Canal, as they connect individual parts of the world ocean and significantly shorten the distances between countries and continents (Szwankowski, 2017, p. 178).

Inland waterway transport involves the transport of goods using inland waterway rolling stock (Jóźwiak, 2011, p. 4727). The linear infrastructure of inland waterway transport, similarly to the maritime transport, is made up of natural land waterways (rivers, lakes) and artificial ones (reservoirs, canals). For rivers and lakes to become navigation routes, they must meet many conditions, including the appropriate depth and width, an appropriate relative drop in water level and a short duration of ice cover presence. It should be emphasized that there are possibilities to adapt river sections that do not fully meet such conditions for navigation, e.g. by canalizing them, or in other words, by grading them, which is the most radical way to improve navigation conditions on the river route. It is mainly used when, on a certain section of the route, the bottom rises too close to the water surface, thus preventing the vessel from passing smoothly. In practice, it involves building barriers (dams or weirs) across the riverbed, which serve to dam up the water and to increase the depth. After the canalization, the waterway acquires a stepped shape, and the individual water levels are called stations. The passage of a vessel from one station to another is carried out using special hydraulic devices (chamber locks) or mechanical devices (slipways, lifts). In addition to ensuring the necessary depth for navigation, canalization can also result in reducing the speed of water in the river (easier navigation against the current), enabling the equalization of flows (extending the navigation period by eliminating interruptions resulting from too low or too high water levels), facilitating the development of adjacent areas, e.g. construction of a port (Wojewódzka-Król, 2008, pp. 97–98).

Many of the rivers currently used for transportation have been transformed into shipping routes through human intervention, already. Moreover, the mere fact that a given section meets certain requirements, either through its natural properties or through human adaptation, does not usually mean that it is exempt from the need to make permanent efforts to maintain it in a state of operational readiness. River and lake navigation routes require numerous, almost continuous technical measures to prevent their erosion. The fact that inland river routes are often created with human involvement and their maintenance requires constant human involvement means that many researchers disagree with the view that they are representative examples of natural routes. They consider them more as a kind of intermediate form, integrating natural and artificial features.

Certainly, typical artificial routes of inland water transport are canals and retention reservoirs. The former are built to supplement or correct the natural network of waterways. Retention reservoirs, in turn, play the role of a tool for improving the navigability of rivers with large differences in flow volume. These reservoirs collect water during periods of flooding, while during periods of low water levels, they feed the river. In this way, they allow for maintaining a relatively constant level of flows on the waterway.

The situation is somewhat different in the case of air transport, which, according to some researchers, lacks linear infrastructure. This approach stems from the nature of the industry's operating environment – airspace. This space can be considered as the main element of linear infrastructure. However, as a road it acquires the characteristics of infrastructure only after the installation of appropriate devices on the ground for air traffic supervision and control, such as radars, communication, or navigation radio stations – they have essentially point-based character. However, it is more common to believe that the linear elements in air transport are air ways, called air corridors (Długosz, Zimniewicz, 2009a, p. 195). They exist vertically and horizontally in the airspace, and only within them aircrafts can move within a specific time period. These airspace segments are divided into:

- national – their width is 10 nautical miles, and they run at an altitude of 900–1200 m (standard altimeter setting);
- international – they run at the same height as national ones, but their width is 20 nautical miles.

The so-called airport-controlled areas connect air ways with airports. These are areas around airports with a radius of several dozen kilometres, where the airport control tower is responsible for communication and traffic management. Controlled areas are usually treated as an element of linear infrastructure (Ruciński, 2007, p. 141).

Point transport infrastructure consists of facilities and devices located on the roads of all modes of transport, necessary for the implementation of transport tasks. These are all types of elements without the presence of which the movement of people and cargo could not take place, because they serve for the needs of people, means of transport during stops or for the service of the transported cargo (material). Similarly to the previously mentioned linear elements, the rest of this subchapter will be devoted to listing and characterizing the elements of point infrastructure of specific transport modes.

Car transport point infrastructure contains spatially separated facilities for stationary service of road transport means, as well as passengers and cargo transported by them. It is divided into passenger one and cargo. Some researchers also distinguish a third type, namely: infrastructure of service of passengers and transport means (Figure 2.7).

The infrastructure elements serving passenger traffic are:

- Stops. These are basic elements of passenger infrastructure. A stop is defined as an appropriately marked place on the road where public transport vehicles stop. Apart from the communication function, a stop also fulfils an information function, resulting from the fact that a timetable is placed there.
- Bus stations. Such units take on the function of stops at transportation hubs. A bus station is understood as a defined area with buildings for passenger service (ticket offices, luggage storage, food, and beverage outlets) and for means of transport service (stations), with arrival and departure stands, bus

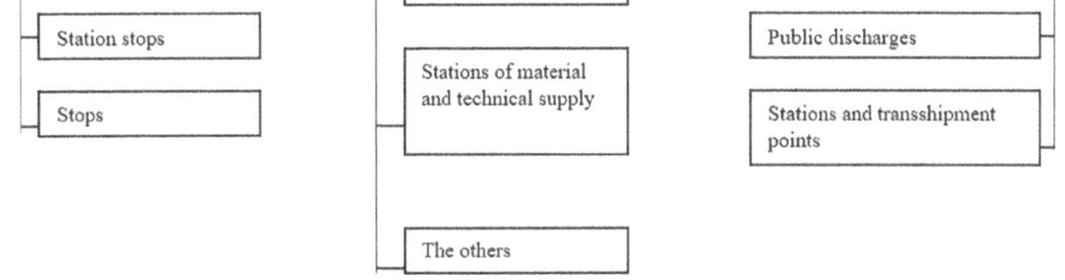

Figure 2.7 Division of car transport's point infrastructure.

Source: Own elaboration based on Wojciechowski, Wojciechowski, Kosmatka (2009).

parking areas and bus service areas (Wojciechowski et al., 2009, p. 233). This definition shows up, that the discussed element of car road transport infrastructure fulfils additional tasks for both passengers and means of transport – compared to a bus stop. Bus stations are expanding their service and commercial functions as passenger traffic intensifies. For the proper functioning of passenger road transport, the most important among them, there are: ticket pre-sale, luggage storage and providing information for travellers, bordering on the promotion of transport services. However, neither commercial nor service functions are the most important among bus stations. The most important is the regulation of bus service. This involves the planned, scheduled dispatch of a larger number of vehicles at a given time, in accordance with a timetable. Bus stations are categorized according to various criteria, e.g. the number of buses dispatched during the day or the type of routes served by the buses dispatched there.

- Station stops. In local public transport, including suburban transport, a specific type of vehicle transport facility has developed called a station stop. It is a grouping of a small number of transfer stops, supplemented with selected infrastructure elements characteristic for bus stations, e.g. a waiting room, ticket offices. The transport of goods by road has led to the development of infrastructure elements aimed at handling the loading, reloading and unloading of transported goods (Szałucki, 2007, p. 43).

The road transport infrastructure supporting cargo transport consists primarily of facilities such as:

- Logistics centres. These are defined as spatial and functional facilities, along with infrastructure and organization, where logistics services related to the receipt, storage, distribution, and issuance of goods are performed, as well as accompanying services provided by economic entities independent to the sender or recipient of goods (Fechner, 2004, p. 14). Logistics centres are therefore de facto outsourcing companies that perform all or selected logistics activities on behalf of the client

(Michalski, 2004, p. 257). The operation of logistics centres is possible thanks to their equipment, which consists of three basic groups of components (Skowron-Grabowska, 2007, p. 38):

a) a limited and separated space together with the infrastructure located therein, including elements such as buildings, parking lots, roads,
b) technological infrastructure used in the storage processes and for handling means of transport,
c) qualified personnel.

Depending on their business profile and customer requirements, logistics centres can perform various functions: from the simplest ones, consisting only of storage, to much more complex ones. For example, some of them operate in the business of accepting deliveries from multiple suppliers, combining them into kits or assembly packages and then handing them over to the manufacturer in accordance with his production plan and schedule. Sometimes they can also act as a nodal point – a hub, which is used when the customer has several points (e.g. production plants or warehouses) and from each of them products are sent to many destinations which are distant from each other. Due to economic reasons, separate means of transport are not sent from each of these points to carry the products to individual locations, but all of them are moved in one transport to the junction point, where they meet all the cargo coming from the other points. There, the entire load is segregated and transshipped in such a way that all goods coming from different points but going to the same destination are transported by one mean of transport. The idea of using nodal points – hubs in logistics comes from the American company Federal Express (Rothman, 2001, pp. 43–44).

- Unloading and transshipment points. These are separate and independently operating elements of the road transport infrastructure, enabling customers to perform specific loading, storage, or cargo-related activities. Therefore, they are equipped with storage space, rolling stock and equipment for transshipment operations. They are divided into public and company-owned.

The infrastructure for servicing means of transport and passengers consists of economic entities of a service nature, which are intended to service means of transport and/or drivers and passengers during the performance of transportation tasks. It consists of elements such as repair and maintenance points (car service stations, car fleet repair plants, technical facilities of road transport companies), material and technical supply stations (petrol stations, car washes, etc.), and finally, points that cannot be classified into any of the previous groups, such as roadside hotels, bars, restaurants, etc. They create road transport infrastructure to the extent that they are responsible for maintaining the technical readiness of the road fleet and to the extent that they are willing to provide their services to the generally accessible road transport services' market. However, the production of these units is now in the nature of maintenance, servicing, overhaul and repair services., so it does not directly create the transport process itself (Szałucki, 2007, p. 43).

Point infrastructure in rail transport consists of spatially separated operational points whose task is to provide stationary passenger and freight services and to conduct train traffic in a punctual and safe manner. Railway stations are an essential element of this infrastructure. The section of railway line between any two stations is called a railway route. Although the movement of passengers and cargo, which is the essence of rail transport, takes place on the railway routes, the results of the entire railway operation depend largely on the proper functioning of the stations where passenger traffic takes place as well as rolling stock manoeuvres and technical service. Railway stations must enable trains to overtake and enable crossing of trains' passages which requires connecting tracks with switches and installing appropriate devices to control traffic. The presence of such equipment distinguishes a railway station from another element of the railway transport infrastructure, such as a passenger stop. It is defined as a place on a route where designated passenger trains stop according to the timetable to allow passengers to board and alight. Although it is prepared to stop passenger trains and board and alight passengers (it has a platform or platforms), at the same time, it does not have track connections with switches and it is not possible to change the order of train movement there (Basiewicz, Gołaszewski, Rudziński, 2007, pp. 59–60).

In addition, railway stations include depots, buildings situated in the railway area, where there are rooms for transport services and there may be rooms for activities related to such services, as well as rooms where activities related to the management of train traffic are carried out.

In the literature, a distinction is made between railway stations. The basic criterion for classification is the type of transport they serve, distinguishing the following types of stations:

- Passenger, intended for servicing passenger trains and the people they transport. They can then be further divided, for example, according to the arrangement of tracks and kind of station buildings,
- Freight, handling the transport of freight shipments. There are three types of them (Figure 2.8),
- passenger and freight, simultaneously performing the tasks of passenger and freight stations.

However, the presented systematics does not fully cover the topic of division of railway stations. Railway stations can also be divided based on various other criteria, such as:

- importance in the rail transportation network. Stations can be designed to handle local, national or international traffic (Neider, 2015, pp. 59–60),

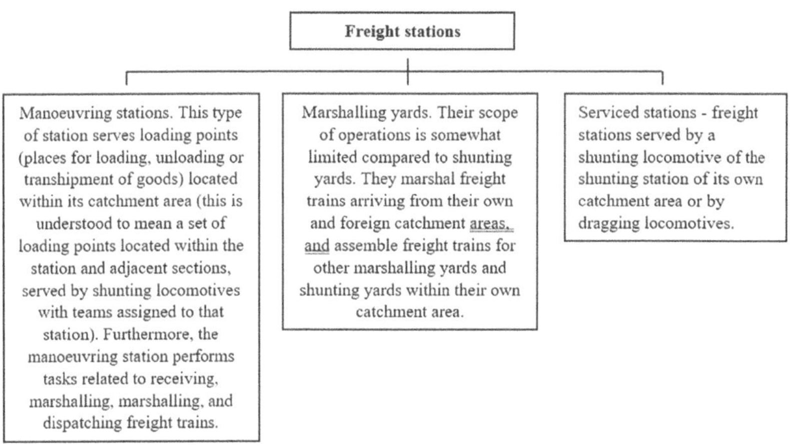

Figure 2.8 Division of freight railway stations.

Source: Own elaboration based on Wojciechowski, Wojciechowski, Kosmatka (2009).

- the type of railway line on which they are located. In this case, such stations are distinguished:
  a) standard gauge,
  b) narrow gauge,
  c) broad gauge,
  d) tangent lines, connecting two different lines, for example standard gauge and narrow gauge.
- the number of railway routes converging at the station. Based on this criterion, stations are divided into junction stations, where at least three routes converge, and non-junction stations, that is, where only one or two routes adjoin,
- working time. Stations are divided into non-stop and periodically open stations. The second group usually includes stations located on lines with low traffic intensity.

Ports, on the other hand, are a key element of maritime transport infrastructure. They are where mass cargo transshipment and passenger traffic take place. These transport hubs are located at the interface between the marine and land environments (Szwankowski, 2017, p. 180). As a result, there are located two complexes: port's aquatorium (the water area of the port) and the land part.

The port's aquatorium includes four components: the port roadstead, the outer port, port channels and basins. The roadstead is the water area of the aquatorium, located outside the breakwater, mainly used for ships to stop while waiting for permission to enter the internal waters of the port, but also for conducting ship inspections, transshipment of hazardous materials, etc. In turn, the outer port is the water area inside the port, separated by a breakwater from the roadstead, where ships entering and leaving the port manoeuvre. Port channels create waterways with appropriate linear hydrotechnical parameters, along which a ship sails to the proper quay. The proper port is constituted with port basins, where ships stop for transshipment and other port services (Figure 2.9).

A large part of the land area of ports is made up of piers, quays, wharfs and breakwaters. A pier is understood as a heavy hydrotechnical structure, with a length that allows for the mooring of at least two ships and a width of 80 to over 200 meters, intended to enable the

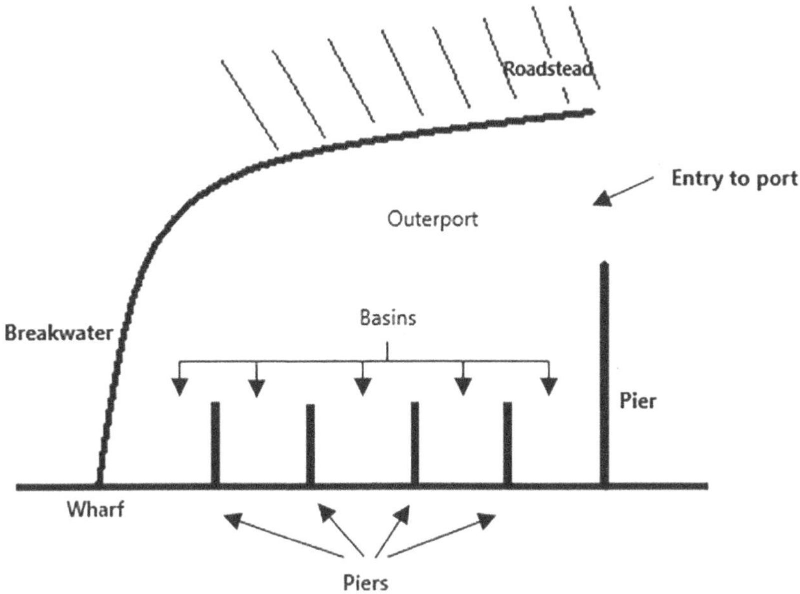

Figure 2.9 Port's aquatorium.

Source: Own elaboration based on Basiewicz, Gołaszewski, Rudziński (2007).

transshipment, storage and dispatch of cargo by land. A pier performs the same tasks, with the proviso that it is a smaller object (width up to 80 meters, length of one ship). A wharf, on the other hand, is the coastline of a pier, basin, and port channel together with the directly adjacent port areas, used for the berthing and handling ships, cargo and passengers. A breakwater is a hydrotechnical structure that protects the port water area from waves, enabling the mooring and reloading of ships (Mendyk, 2009, p. 79).

The port's land area includes passenger terminals, administrative buildings, warehouses, control rooms, storage yards, various installation systems and specialist transshipment equipment. In addition, ports are crossed by rail and car roads. They are often also connected to inland waterways. Ports are linked with the infrastructure of other transport sectors to jointly provide transport services.

Similarly to maritime water transport, in inland waterway transport, the basic element of point infrastructure are ports, where not only cargo and passenger handling is performed, but also repairs, maintenance and modernization of ships.

According to researchers, a river port is a water area (aquarium) and land area (territory) defined by a border, where – thanks to appropriate equipment – transshipment from land transport means to a river vessel or vice versa takes place as well as the broadly understood handling of cargo, ships and means of transport for incoming and outgoing cargo (Galińska et al. 1992, p. 77). This definition highlights the fact that river ports are primarily used for transshipment of goods. It should be noted, however, that in inland navigation, apart from commercial ports, which are actually built for this purpose, there are also so-called winter ports, which serve solely to anchor vessels during the period when inland waterways are closed due to unfavourable weather and climatic conditions (e.g. they are frozen).

River ports, depending on their functions and location, are characterized by very diverse sizes. They are usually smaller than seaports, but their infrastructure consists of practically the same elements (Wojewódzka-Król, 2008, p. 103). Thus, the basic components of the river port aquatorium include: the roadstead, the outer port, port channels and basins. On the other hand, its land area includes quays, breakwaters, piers, jetties, storage yards, warehouses, unloading facilities, transport routes in the port area, buildings as well as other built-up port areas.

Similarly, air transport can only take place between appropriately adapted transport points. These include airports and ports. They are absolutely necessary for the performance of air transport. While in other branches of transport, in extreme emergency situations, it is possible to accept and service a means of transport outside designated and appropriately prepared transport points (ports, stations, stops), in air transport, due to the technical specificity of the branch, this is practically impossible (Ruciński, 2007, p. 141).

An airfield is a designated area on land, water or other surface, in whole or in part intended for take-off, landing and ground or water movement of aircrafts, together with the permanent structures and construction facilities located within its boundaries, entered in the register of airfields. On the other hand, an airport is a fully equipped public airfield that additionally has the facilities necessary to perform tasks resulting from commercial passenger transport. Based on a comparison of these definitions, it can be stated that every airport is an airfield, but not every airfield is an airport (e.g. military, because it does not perform commercial functions for the civilian population). The airport therefore has additional functions compared to the airfield. Commercial operations related to the sale of aviation, passenger and cargo services are carried out there. It is also worth noting that despite the above-mentioned differences between an airfield and an airport, both terms can be used interchangeably not only in everyday language but also in the literature on the subject, and this is often done by treating them as synonyms.

The third component of air transport point infrastructure are landing sites, which, like airport, are also areas designated for take-offs, landings and ground movement of aircraft, included in the register. The distinction between landing sites and airfields or airports does not therefore concern the functions they perform, but rather corresponds to the historical development of the concept of an air transport point (in the early days of aviation, landing sites were used, with the development of this field, airfields appeared, and later, with the growing importance of commercial functions – airports) and, in modern times, to the various scope of services provided by these points (Ruciński, 2007, p. 141). In the early days of air transport, each point element of its infrastructure was usually a grass runway and a few tents (Nahum, 1996, s. 32). Nowadays, the airport covers an area of several thousand hectares (e.g. Denver International Airport (DIA) stretches across a staggering 135.69 square kilometres (52.4 square miles) – that's an area larger than the size of Manhattan and Brooklyn combined (Mwaniki, 2025), on which there is a diverse type of construction objects. Each of them can be classified as a part of one of the two basic land components of the airport:

- Ground movement area. Its main part is the manoeuvring area, where aircraft movement related to take-off and landing takes place. The part of the manoeuvring area adapted for take-offs and landings is the take-off area. The most important facilities located there include runways, airport aprons (used for commercial and technical service of the air fleet), taxiways that connect runways with airport aprons, technical and radiotechnical installations used to safely guide aircraft along the prescribed route during take-off, approach to landing and landing.

- Port building, which includes:

  a) a passenger station with areas for customs and passport control, waiting rooms and communication corridors, rooms for security control services and service facilities (catering, commercial, etc.).
  b) a freight station with rooms for customs and trade services, forwarders, agents, institutions related to cargo handling, e.g. veterinary ones,
  c) cargo warehouses equipped with handling equipment for short-term storage of shipments before loading them onto aircraft, completing group shipments, forming cargo units, etc.
  d) technical facilities (e.g. hangars, repair workshops, warehouses for operating parts) and administrative as well as economic facilities,
  e) a traffic control centre (control tower), which, thanks to radar and signalling devices, ensures the reception of aircraft both during the day and at night, even in difficult weather conditions.

There are state, municipal, and private airports. Depending on the size and intensity of air traffic, they have character of:

- international. They handle scheduled and non-scheduled international flights, providing them with full inspection, customs and immigration services and enabling contact with local authorities. Such airports must meet all the requirements and recommendations of the International Civil Aviation Organization (ICAO),
- Regional. Large facilities serving scheduled and non-scheduled flights in domestic traffic and non-scheduled flights in international (regional) traffic. They also serve business flights, private aircraft operations and cargo transport. They can also serve as alternate airports for international airports.
- Secondary ones, which usually do not serve scheduled flights, but rather tourist, commercial, business and private traffic.

The above-mentioned airports are supplemented by the network of small, general aviation airports, which constitute the area of operations for non-unloading general aviation flights, a place for possible forced landings of general aviation aircrafts, place for air training and sports activities. They usually do not have many and paved runways (Ruciński, 2007, p. 145).

2.4 Means of Transport Being Used

In the subsection 2.2 of this monograph, the branches and types of modern transport have been discussed. In connection with these issues, in this subsection we will focus on the analysis of means of transport currently used in ITS. They will be characterized primarily from the perspective of greening them, because the usage of environmentally friendly transport solutions is one of the key elements of modern mobility systems.

The use of ecological means of transport in ITS allows for a significant reduction in the emission of harmful greenhouse gases, a reduction in the level of air pollution and noise, which directly translates into an improvement in the quality of life of residents, protection of the natural environment and the implementation of sustainable development goals. The concept of sustainable development plays an important role in shaping the directions of development of ITS, promoting solutions that take into account the balance between economic, social and ecological needs.

In practice, this means that sustainable development requires the design and implementation of transport systems that are safe, accessible to various groups of users, energy-efficient and climate-neutral. It promotes the popularization of technologies that reduce exhaust emissions, improve traffic flow, support public transport and the development of shared mobility, which in turn is to contribute to the creation of a more sustainable and fair transport system. As can be assessed, only environmentally friendly means of transport will be used in the future, which at the same time demonstrate a high, uniform level of safety and connectivity. Implementing sustainable development solutions into practice is today a key issue for all types of transport. The current drive systems are no longer suitable, because they have a negative impact on the natural environment and human health.

Transport-related factors that particularly burden planet are air pollution and noise, leading to climate change and the destruction of natural ecosystems. In the European Union, transport is the source of almost 54% of total emissions of nitrogen oxides, 45% of carbon monoxide, 23% of non-methane volatile organic compounds, 23% of PM10 and 28% of PM2.5 (particulate matter with a diameter of 10 and 2.5 μm, respectively). It is also responsible for over 41% of tropospheric ozone precursor emissions, 23% of carbon dioxide emissions and almost 20% of other greenhouse gases (Merkisz, 2024). The largest share in greenhouse gas emissions in Europe in 2022 was accounted for by road transport (73.18%), followed by water transport (14.23%) and air transport (11.77%), and the smallest by rail transport (0.33%) and other means of transport (0.49%) (Urząd Transportu Kolejowego, 2025). On the other hand, according to the US Environmental Protection Agency (EPA), emissions from the transportation sector increased by 29% between 1990 and 2006. The main reasons were the increase in transportation needs and the stagnation of fuel efficiency indicators used in American cars (Cieślakowski, 2011, pp. 78–83).

The noise levels generated by individual modes of transport are generally too low to cause hearing damage. However, long-term exposure to sounds above a certain level can lead to so-called non-auditory health effects, in extreme cases, even to cognitive impairment (Orczyk, 2024). It has been scientifically proven what negative effects noise has on humans. It leads to problems with sleep, concentration, and moreover causes stress, depression, headaches, dizziness and many others (Pabian, Pabian, Bilińska, 2025, p. 55). In the context of global efforts to protect the environment and combat climate change, the modern, eco-innovative solutions discussed in this subsection, being taken from all modes of transport, will contribute to limit the scale and scope of negative effects resulting from mass communication. They may concern design solutions of means of transport, modification of vehicles' combustion systems or load preparation systems or the use of eco-fuel.

I Car transport. Although the name of the branch suggests which means of transport are mainly included in it, apart from motor vehicles, also non-motor vehicles travel on its roads. Among motor vehicles, the following stand out:

a) vehicles for passenger transport (individual – mopeds, motorcycles, scooters, passenger cars as well as public – buses),
b) vehicles for cargo transport (with universal bodywork – vans, tarpaulin-covered boxes and with specialized bodywork adapted to transport non-standard loads – refrigerated trucks, tippers, tankers, for transporting animals, etc.),
c) special vehicles, equipped with special devices and intended to perform specific work (ambulances, fire trucks, roadside assistance),
d) truck tractors (semi-trailers, ballast tractors).

Among non-engine vehicles, the following stand out:

a) bikes,
b) trailers,
c) semi-trailers.

Automotive companies, focusing on decarbonizing the transport sector and promoting low-emission transport are increasingly presenting eco-solutions in car transport, which enable more efficient usage of fuel and minimize exhaust emissions. Systems such as energy recovery, automatic engine shutdown when stationary (start-stop), and intelligent drive management help to achieve it. This is the right development path, because, as can be judged, combustion engines, due to their efficiency, are expected to remain the main power source for road transport vehicles for a long time to come. Changes may also be made to the fuel being used. Conventional fuels are currently being replaced by hydrocarbon gas fuels (including methane) and fuels that do not contain carbon in their molecules (hydrogen, ammonia) as well as by synthetic fuels. The use of all these fuels allows, among other things, for lean charge combustion, which, according to theory, increases the efficiency of combustion engines (Pielecha, 2024). High-pressure combustion systems for light hydrocarbon (liquid) fuels are designed to increase fuel pressure, which promotes greater fuel atomization, leading to an increased rate of fuel charge formation. Turbulent jet ignition (TJI) is an example of a modern combustion system based on the combustion of lean mixtures. Its essence consists of two chambers: the preliminary chamber, which is used to initiate ignition and burn the initial dose of fuel, and the main chamber. Burning fuel flames flow from the pre-chamber to the main chamber, enabling the lean charge in the main chamber to ignite. The active system has an injector in the pre-chamber that doses fuel to this chamber, while the passive system lacks an additional injector, and charge ignitability is achieved by fuel flow from the main chamber (Pielecha, 2024).

Manufacturers also improve the aerodynamics of the body, increase the gear ratios or use systems that allow the engine to be temporarily turned off when the car is stationary, which is useful in traffic jams (BlueDrive Hyundai; EcoDynamics Kia). They reduce weight and use tires with reduced rolling resistance. Combined with an economical, small engine (usually diesel type), this minimizes fuel consumption for a given car model. This is all thanks to the use of a complex catalytic reactor and the addition of a high-purity 32.5% aqueous urea solution (so-called: AdBlue, which decomposes into ammonia in the hot exhaust stream, neutralizing nitrogen oxides).

Reducing harmful emissions and fuel consumption is also achieved through computer software and factory chip tuning, but this time focused on reducing fuel consumption (Seat, VW). BMW uses a braking energy recovery solution. By converting energy from the vehicle's brakes into electricity, it can be used to charge the battery, which is then independent of the engine, reducing fuel consumption. In turn, the Volvo cars manufacturer, in the XC60 and XC70 models, uses only front-wheel drive instead of the AWD system known from these models, which results in very low fuel consumption (Autokult, 2025).

Such solutions, to a greater or lesser extent, but are already used in cars of many brands. Examples of eco-friendly passenger cars include the Audi Q7 Clean Diesel, which reduces fuel consumption by 0.2 litres in city driving. Although CO2 emissions remain the same, CO2 is broken down into nitrogen and water vapour. Volkswagen is promoting its BlueMotion series models, Skoda – Greenline models, Seat (EcoMotive), Hyundai (BlueDrive), Kia (EcoDynamics), Volvo (DRIVe), and Citroën (eHDI).

In road transport, increasingly eco-friendly combustion engines coexist with hybrid and electric ones. The former technology represents a significant step towards more sustainable transport and is often considered a transitional stage between traditional combustion vehicles and fully electric vehicles. Hybrid drive in cars is a solution that combines a combustion engine with an electric engine, which aims to increase vehicle's energy efficiency and to reduce exhaust emissions. Conversely, there are also electric vehicles equipped with an additional combustion engine that, operating at optimal speeds, recharges the batteries. Thanks to the cooperation of both powertrains, hybrid cars consume less fuel, especially in urban environments where frequent stops and starts allow for optimal use of the electric engine.

Generally, there are three types of hybrid drives: serial, parallel and mixed, which differ in the way the electric motor is connected to the combustion engine. In a serial drive, the combustion engine acts as a generator that drives the electric motor. In this construction, the task of driving the wheels is assigned to the electric unit. When the battery is discharged, the combustion engine turns on and drives the generator, which recharges the battery. In addition, in a serial connection, energy is also obtained during braking. In the parallel hybrid drive variant, the combustion engine and the electric motor are both mechanically connected to the wheels. The vehicle can be powered by either a combustion engine or an electric engine alone, or both at the same time. The electric motors are designed to add torque during acceleration and recover energy during braking. In the case of a serial-parallel drive, the efficiency of the serial system at low speeds and the savings of the parallel system at higher speeds are taken advantage of. The operation of both engines also depends on the driving style. Relatively short distances can be covered solely using the electric motor what eliminates fuel consumption. Many Toyota models are good examples of hybrid vehicles, including, among others, Toyota RAV4 Hybrid (Kujda, Pawlak, 2020, pp. 67–78).

Purely electric cars are an increasingly important part of the modern automotive market, offering an environmentally friendly alternative to traditional combustion vehicles. Thanks to their electrical power, they emit no exhaust fumes while driving, they contribute to noise reduction and improved air quality, among other things. Technological progress, the development of charging infrastructure and growing support from countries and international institutions are contributing to the popularization of this type of drive, although it should be emphasized that electric cars still face many challenges, such as limited range, charging time, the risk of ignition, high purchase and service costs as well as difficulties in neutralizing used batteries. Independent electric drive using batteries can be implemented according to two concepts. In the plug-in system, the batteries are boosted, which requires a longer stop and, above all, an increase in the number of stations and eco-power points for these vehicles is necessary. In an alternative version, the batteries can be replaced with a new set under special conditions – so an appropriate infrastructure is also required for this. The latest examples of such eco-friendly vehicles include electric vehicles such as the Tesla Model Y, Volkswagen ID.4 and Ford Mustang Mach-E (Cieślakowski, 2011, pp. 78–83).

Despite the development of pure electric vehicles, the authorities of many cities, including the Spanish city of Barcelona, are relying on alternative technologies. Implementing a sustainable urban transport program, this city initially focused on buses powered by CNG (Compressed Natural Gas), later replacing them with hybrids. Currently, in addition to the standard methane-powered unit, these buses are equipped with two electric traction motors, ultracapacitors for energy storage, what is more – a braking energy recovery system and other hybrid system components. It uses electric motors with a power output of 75 kW each and a torque of 3,000 Nm. This solution reduces noise emissions thanks to quiet starting and a smooth, even ride (Jóźwiak, 2015, pp. 1–23).

It's worth noting that hybrid buses are generally becoming quite common in European Union countries. Above all, vehicle's design allows for the integration of hybrid drive system components, such as batteries, capacitors, and cooling systems, on the vehicle's roof, without compromising passenger space. The most important elements of a hybrid drive are: an internal combustion engine, an electric motor, a microprocessor system, a gearbox, energy storage devices and, in some solutions, generators.

Examples of environmentally friendly freight transport include, among others, hybrid Scania, hybrid MAN, Scania burning LNG, CNG bus, and the electric Volkswagen Crafter. In 2023, during the NUFAM trade fair in Karlsruhe, Germany, as part of the European Truck Challenge test comparing long-distance trucks from three brands: Scania, DAF and Mercedes, the Scania 420 R tractor unit has been awarded in the category of the most fuel-efficient vehicle. Modern and ecological drivetrain with the recently improved Active Prediction cruise control contributed significantly to the victory (SCANIA Poland, 2025).

The development of completely emission-free, electric freight transport could be achieved in the future, among other things, by using overhead power supply technology. Collecting power via a pantograph while driving reduces the size of trucks' batteries and, above all, bypasses the problem of powering chargers' absence. In 2019, already, two sections of five kilometres each were tested in Germany as a part of the eHighway Lubeck project. (eHighway.SH, 2025).

Modern trolleybuses, in turn, increasingly use supercapacitors, which allow for the recuperation of braking energy, which is then fed back to the grid. A current-carrying cable is placed in the street beneath the trolleybus track. This creates a magnetic field, and the air gap between the vehicle and the track containing the cable must be 70-100 mm. This technology can be also used for trams, where the cable is laid between the rails, and for electric buses, where the cable is laid under the street Surface (Cieślakowski, 2011, pp. 78–83).

II Air transport. We distinguish between civil aviation and military aviation. Air transport's means include:

a) aircrafts, differing in design, size, propulsion, range, speed and purpose, used for various aims: transporting people, cargo, monitoring the situation on the ground, reconnaissance and combating targets, transporting troops and supplies, conducting scientific research and experiments,
b) helicopters capable of vertical take-off and landing, used for transporting people and cargo over short distances, in medical rescue, firefighting, police patrols, border control, military reconnaissance, fire support and so on,
c) blimps, capable of rising into the air using a balloon filled with helium or hydrogen,
d) drones – unmanned aerial vehicles (UAVs) – flying devices that are remotely controlled or operate autonomously based on programmed routes and sensors. Although not yet

widespread, more advanced ones can be used to transport small payloads over short distances,

e) gliders are aircrafts without engine propulsion that hover in the air using aerodynamic forces and natural atmospheric phenomena. Their typically lightweight and slender design enables long-lasting and quiet flights, often over considerable distances. Gliding is not only a form of recreation and sport, but also a form of training – many pilots begin their aviation adventures in gliders. Thanks to the ability to fly without an engine, gliding is considered one of the most ecologically clean forms of aviation.

f) space shuttles, designed to transport crews and cargo between Earth and the space stations.

The importance of air transport for the global economy, including tourism, international trade and investment is fundamental. According to forecasts, in the next two decades, that is, by 2041, air transport will increase 2.3-fold, and airlines will purchase 41,200 aircraft (worth $7.2 trillion), according to Boeing, and 39,500 units – according to Airbus (Liwiński, 2025). In alike manner, IATA (International Air Transport Association) forecasts that over the next two decades the number of passengers using air transport in the world will be growing at an average annual rate of 3.8%, which translates into almost 8 billion travellers in 2043 (Dybiński, Malinowski, 2024). Given these projections, the real challenge is to increase and ensure fuel efficiency while eliminating the carbon footprint. Numerous initiatives are underway to accelerate research and innovation in engine and airframe technologies, key to reducing CO2 emissions in aviation. For example, the EU-led Clean Aviation Joint Undertaking, a research and innovation initiative aims to accelerate aviation's transition towards climate neutrality. It operates under Horizon Europe and follows on from the earlier so-called Clean Sky programme. It focuses on developing breakthrough technologies for new generations of aircraft, including hybrid, electric and hydrogen propulsion systems, which are expected to significantly reduce CO_2 emissions, noise and fossil fuel consumption in European aviation by 2050. In turn, the SESAR 3 Joint Undertaking Programme aims to digitalize the European sky, which will improve air traffic management and reduce fuel consumption (Majka, 2024).

Far-reaching solutions for green aviation include a shift to innovative propulsion systems and sustainable, zero-emission aviation fuels, including the usage of hydrogen, both through direct combustion in engines and through hydrogen fuel cells. Although it is not currently widely used, CO2 emission reduction in aviation can be achieved through the usage of hybrid or purely electric drives as well as biofuels or synthetic fuels. However, electric and hybrid drives require breakthroughs in battery technology and energy storage systems. In turn, the production of biofuels and synthetic fuels must be ecologically sustainable.

Sustainable Aviation Fuel (SAF) is currently derived from renewable, non-fossil feedstocks, including waste streams such as used cooking oil. While SAF emits the same amount of CO_2 during flight, its entire lifecycle (from production to combustion) reduces its CO_2 impact by at least 65%. It also reduces other harmful emissions, such as particulate matter and sulphur. Unfortunately, SAF is three to ten times more expensive than conventional fuel. However, to protect the environment, some airlines are increasing their SAF usage by adding a small amount to the fuel system, making up 0.5% of the fuel used on each flight. The plan is to gradually increase this amount to an average of 1% (KLM Royal Dutch Airlines, 2025).

Experts point out that among the constraints on clean aviation are not only the high prices of sustainable aviation fuel and limited capacity to produce it, but also supply chain problems that delay the renewal of the fleet of aircrafts that would be capable of running on it (Zrównoważone nie zrównoważone, 2025).

The world's first zero-emission aircraft is planned to be Airbus ZEROe, powered by hydrogen, which will be converted into electricity in fuel cells, powering electric motors. The only byproduct will be water. The aircraft will have four propellers, each powered by its own fuel cell stack. The Airbus ZEROe is expected to enter service in 2035. The hydrogen, being used must be produced in the process of electrolysis with the usage of renewable energy. Currently, however, the demand for renewable hydrogen (so-called: green hydrogen) significantly exceeds the supply, because its modern production is not yet very profitable. Furthermore, whether hydrogen is burned directly or converted into electricity in fuel cells, it must be safely stored at a temperature of – 253 degrees of Celsius. Today, already, expert teams are working together to design and produce innovative cryogenic storage systems that will enable hydrogen-powered flights. The Hydrogen Hubs at Airports project has been launched, with over 220 airports signing up (AIRBUS, 2025).

III. Rail transport – heavy loads are transported by rail over long distances, and the longer the distance, the lower the unit transport costs. The list of conventional rail transport's means includes:

a) locomotives, i.e. rail vehicles used to pull trains, powered by traditional diesel engines, electricity or using magnetism,
b) railway wagons (open platform and mineral freight wagons; closed tank and covered freight wagons; specialized wagons for transporting cars or containers; wagons for transporting dangerous goods; wagons for transporting animals; passenger wagons, including sleeping cars, restaurant wagons, open-space wagons), consisting of a platform, chassis, axles and wheels as well as a system of springs and shock absorbers that ensure comfortable and safe movement of loads or passengers.

Rail transport is an efficient and competitive way to move big amount of freight away from congested car roads, improving traffic flow and reducing vehicles' emissions (Włudyka & Orłowski, 2009, pp. 70–76).

The rail industry's share of greenhouse gas emissions is the smallest among all other modes of transport. Some locomotives are diesel-powered, but in Europe, environmental concerns have led to stricter emission limits for nitrogen oxides and solid particles for engines in mobile rail-based machinery. Combustion rail vehicles belong to the NRMM (Non-Road Mobile Machinery) group, which includes mobile machines running on rails, including: building equipment, construction dumpers, power generators, forestry machines, agricultural machines, chainsaws and others. According to European requirements, newly manufactured rail vehicles must comply with the Stage V standard. It requires usage of DPF filters (diesel particulate filters) for engines with power ranging from 19 to 560 kW. In order to achieve lower emissions of harmful substances, the following systems are used: DOC (Diesel Oxidation Catalyst), DPF (Diesel Particulate Filter), DEF (Diesel Exhaust Fluid), SCR (Selective Catalytic Reduction), ASC

(Ammonia Slip Catalyst). The use of a DOC oxidizes HC, CO, and some of the particulate matter. The DPF, in turn, reduces the concentration of particulate matter in the exhaust gas. AdBlue is then injected for catalytic reduction in the SCR to reduce NOx emissions. The last element of the system is an ammonia leak catalyst, which is designed to reduce NH3 emissions leaking from the SCR (Daszkiewicz, 2024).

Among the new solutions in the railway industry, the idea of using a dynamic brake is worth noting, as it allows for reducing the wear of brake friction pairs and thus reducing dust emissions resulting from the interaction of brake discs and pads. Applying braking activates the traction motors to operate as generators. This induces voltage, and the energy generated creates drag, which reduces travel speed.

The railway industry, while still dominated by combustion and traction drives, is also experimenting with completely new power sources. An example of a modern vehicle is the Coradia iLint, powered by hydrogen. The fuel cells are located on the roof, and the lithium-ion battery is under the vehicle's floor. The vehicle does not have an internal combustion engine, so it can be used to achieve zero emissions. Such a vehicle could operate on non-electrified traction. Hydrogen fuel cells are characterized by a simple principle of operation, negligible emissions of harmful substances and relatively high electrical efficiency, which for typical cells is in the range of 40–60%, and the overall efficiency can reach 80–90% when generating electrical energy (Daszkiewicz, 2024). However, hydrogen locomotives are still a thing of the future. Currently, the most intense work is on hybrid vehicles combining traditional drive types (diesel and electric) with modern hydrogen as an intermediate link on the path to zero-emission vehicles, or alternatively, there are developed and modernized well-known technologies.

An example of a dual-drive locomotive is the Pesa Gama 111DE. This eco-friendly locomotive minimizes maintenance costs. It can be used for both freight trains at speeds of up to 140 km/h and passenger trains at speeds of up to 160 km/h. Other vehicles in this category include: a shunting locomotive with a hydrogen drive – the result of the modernization of the SM42-6Dn Hydrogen locomotive (it is the first stage of the PESA program for the implementation of hydrogen technologies in rail vehicle drives), the Gama Marathon 111Ed range (an electric locomotive with a diesel shunting engine), the Gama Diesel 111Db range (it has a modern drive with one liquid-cooled traction converter and two two-level inverters for each traction bogie separately. It is equipped with an electrodynamic and resistance brake. The tractive force is transferred from the bogies to the body using inclined traction rods), Gama Electric 111Eb (it has a modern drive with two liquid-cooled traction converters and four inverters, one for each traction motor. It is equipped with an electrodynamic regenerative and resistance brake. The tractive force is transferred from the bogies to the body using inclined traction rods), Gama Multisystem 111Ms (its reinforced cabin cage, made of the highest quality steel, guarantees the safety of the driver). During a collision, the coupler first absorbs the force of the impact, while energy absorbers play a key role, not only absorbing the energy but also preventing the vehicles from climbing over each other. In the second phase, the impact energy is absorbed by the so-called honeycomb – a block of specially shaped aluminium elements. The scraper mounted under the cabin prevents any elements from getting under the vehicle's wheels (PESA, 2025).

As can be seen, innovative and environmentally friendly solutions are being introduced in the railway industry. The most important specific conditions in the scope of the possibilities of their implementation relate to the intended use of vehicles and the availability of electrified railway lines.

IV. Water transport. As detailed in subsection 2.2., water transport is divided into maritime and inland and involves delivering cargo or transporting people via sea or inland waterways for commercial purposes. Means of water transport include:

a) passenger ships used for the transport of people at sea or inland waters (cruise ships, ferries, catamarans),
b) container ships, used to transport cargo in standard metal containers,
c) gas tankers used to transport liquefied natural gas or refined gas,
d) bulk carriers, used to transport large quantities of homogeneous, loose cargo,
e) general cargo ships used to transport packaged cargo that does not require special transport conditions,

f) tankers for transporting liquid cargo,
g) ro-ro ships, i.e. roll-on/roll-off ships, used for the transportation of rolling cargo and vehicles over short and medium distances along the coast, between ports in different countries, equipped with ramps or platforms that allow drivers of various means of transport to enter and exit the ship's deck, without the need to use cranes or overhead cranes,
h) tugboats intended for manoeuvring and towing other vessels,
i) river barges, used to transport cargo on rivers and canals,
j) river boats used in inland navigation, both for the transport of goods and passengers,
k) patrol boats intended for the monitoring and maintaining security,
l) rescue units.

Researchers point out that currently over 80% of all world trade is carried out with the usage of ships. In 2021, the global fleet numbered over 100,000 vessels. Cargo ships (bulk carriers, tankers, chemical tankers, general cargo ships – including container ships) account for 62% of the total fleet, with the rest consisting mainly of passenger and passenger-vehicle ferries, cruise ships, offshore vessels, tugboats and dredgers (Kniaziewicz, 2024).

Almost all of these ships are powered by fossil fuels and ship engines emit in huge quantities, in addition to carbon dioxide (CO2), such toxic substances as sulphur oxides (SOx), nitrogen oxides (NOx), carbon monoxide (CO), unburned hydrocarbons (HC), and particulate matter (PM). However, despite the high costs, modern shipping is increasingly striving to introduce more ecological means of transport, responding to global challenges related to environmental protection and climate change. The shipping industry has committed not only to ambitious CO2 emission reduction targets, but also to the complete decarbonization of international maritime transport as soon as possible after 2050. The plan is to use ammonia, hydrogen and batteries to power the global fleet (International Chamber of Shipping, 2020). As in other sectors, new sources of energy and types of fuels are emerging in shipping such as batteries and fuel cells, biofuels, hydrogen and green ammonia, synthesized in a catalytic reaction of nitrogen and hydrogen under high pressure and temperature as well as methanol, which produces water and carbon dioxide during combustion. Emissions can also be reduced by simply reducing the speed of ships, increasing the share of vessels partially powered by wind or solar energy, or using liquefied natural gas (LNG). French logistics and shipping group CMA CGM has become a pioneer in the use of LNG for container ships. Similarly, Danish shipping company Maersk revealed that it has contracted eight 16,000-TEU container ships from Hyundai Heavy Industries, powered by green methanol, for its operations (SEALAND Group, 2025).

References

AIRBUS webpage. (2025), *ZEROe: our hydrogen-powered aircraft. Developing our first hydrogen-powered commercial aircraft:* www.airbus.com/en/innovation/energy-transition/hydrogen/zeroe-our-hydrogen-powered-aircraft.

Akumulator.pl. (2025), Liczba samochodów na świecie: www.akumulator.pl/artykuly/liczba-samochodow-na-swiecie/.

Andrzejewska S., Kamyszek K., Merkisz-Guranowska A. (2013), *Identyfikacja czynników determinujących atrakcyjność środków transportu*, *Technika Transportu Szynowego*, vol. 20, no. 10, 1029–1038.

Autokult. (2025), Ekologiczne wersje popularnych pojazdów: https://autokult.pl/ekologiczne-wersje-popularnych-pojazdow,6808041244059777a.

Basiewicz T., Gołaszewski A., Rudziński L. (2007), *Infrastruktura transportu*, Warszawa: Oficyna Wydawnicza Politechniki Warszawskiej.

Brill J., Łukasik Z. (2024), *Aspekty ekonomiczne, techniczne i strategiczne transportu intermodalnego*, *Technika Transportu Szynowego*, vol. 21, no. 3, 12–24.

Brzezińska J. (2021), *Transport drogowy i zdrowie*, HEAL Polska: 2021chrome-extension://efaidnbmnnnibpcajpcglclefindmkaj/ https://healpolska.pl/wp-content/uploads/2021/12/Transport-drogowy-i-zdrowie_broszura-HEAL.pdf.

Ciesielski M. (2006), *Transport w logistyce*, [in:] *Kompendium wiedzy o logistyce*, Gołembska E. (eds.), Warszawa: PWN.

Cieślakowski S. J. (2011), *Ekologia w transporcie samochodowym*, Autobust. *Technika, Eksploatacja, Systemy Transportowe*, vol. 12, no. 12, 78–83.

Czermański E. (2011), *Zagadnienia terminologiczne transportu wielogałęziowego*, *Contemporary Economy Electronic Scientific Journal*, vol. 2, no. 2, 47–53.

Daszkiewicz P. (2024), *Ekologia w transporcie kolejowym*, Polskie forum transportu, logistyki i spedycji, 27-28 czerwca 2024 r.

Dąbrowski A., Stencel G. (2016), *Rodzaje nawierzchni na przejazdach kolejowo-drogowych i ich wprowadzanie do obrotu*, Zeszyty Naukowo-Techniczne Stowarzyszenia Inżynierów i Techników Komunikacji Rzeczpospolitej Polskiej, *Oddział w Krakowie*, vol. 2, no. 109, 47–68.

Demeyer S., Audenaert P., Pickavet M., Demeester P. (2014), *Dynamic and stochastic routing for multimodal transportation systems*, *IET Intelligent Transport Systems*, vol. 8, no. 2, 112–123.

Długosz J., Zimniewicz S. (2009a), *Współczesne technologie w transporcie*, [in:] *Nowoczesne technologie w logistyce*, Długosz J. (eds.), Warszawa: PWE.

Długosz J., Zimniewicz S. (2009b), *Żegluga śródlądowa*, [in:] *Nowoczesne technologie w logistyce,* Długosz J. (eds.), Warszawa: PWE.

Długosz M., Roman M., Węgrzyn P. (2021), *System sterowania autonomicznego pojazdu a-eve, Przegląd Elektrotechniczny*, vol. 97, no. 8, 42–47.

Duan R. (2023), *A comparative study on ITS (intelligent transport system) standardization policies in the U.S. and Europe*, *Heliyon*, vol. 9, no. 1, 1–17.

Dybiński R., Malinowski Ł. (2024), *Pasażer i linie lotnicze. IATA: Za dwie dekady niemal 8 mld podróżnych. Kluczowy jeden region*, Rynek Lotniczy: www.rynek-lotniczy.pl/wiadomosci/iata-za-dwie-dekady-niemal-8-mld-podroznych-kluczowy-jeden-region-22828.html.

Directive 2010/40/EU of the European Parliament and of the Council of 7 July 2010 on the framework for the deployment of Intelligent Transport Systems in the field of road transport and on interfaces with other modes of transport: https://eur-lex.europa.eu/legal-content/PL/TXT/?uri=CELEX%3A32010L0040.

eHighway. (2025), *SH ehighway*: https://ehighway-sh.de/der-ehighway-in-schleswig-holstein-ist-betriebsbereit/.

Encyklopedia zarządzania. (2025), *Inteligentne systemy transportowe*: https://mfiles.pl/pl/index.php/Inteligentne_systemy_transportowe.

European Conference of Ministers of Transport. (2004)., *Assessment & decision making for sustainable transport*, Paris: OECD Publications Service.

European Union Aviation Safety Agency (2025), Europejski raport z 2025 r. dotyczący wpływu lotnictwa na środowisko: www.easa.europa.eu/pl/light/topics/european-aviation-environmental-report-2025.

Fechner I. (2004), *Centra logistyczne. Cel, realizacja, przyszłość*, Poznań: Biblioteka Logistyka.

Fertsch M. (2006), *Słownik terminologii logistycznej*, Poznań: Biblioteka Logistyka.

Ficoń K. (2009), *Logistyka techniczna. Infrastruktura logistyczna*, Warszawa: BEL Studio.

Galińska H., Wojewódzka-Król K. (1992), *Technologia śródlądowego transportu wodnego*, Gdańsk: Wydawnictwo Uniwersytetu Gdańskiego.

García-Ortiz A., Amin S. M., Wootton J. R. (1995), *Intelligent transportation systems – enabling technologies*, *Mathematical and Computer Modelling: An International Journal*, vol. 22, no. 4–7, 11–87.

Gołembska E. (2009), *Logistyka w gospodarce światowej*, Warszawa: Wydawnictwo C. H. Beck.

Gołembska E., Szymczak M. (2004), *Logistyka międzynarodowa*, Warszawa: PWE.

Górowski M. (2025), Transport Szynowy: www.transportszynowy.pl/Tramwaje/torytrambezpodsypka

Grzybowska K. (2009), *Podstawy logistyki*, Warszawa: Difin.

Instytut Rozwoju Myśli Ekologicznej. (2017), *Optymalizacja środków transportu*: https://irme.pl/optymalizacja-srodkow-transportu/.

International Chamber of Shipping. (2020), *Catalysing the fourth propulsion revolution*, London: Marisec Publications.

Jędrzejczyk W. (2024), Sharing economy – access is better than ownership: Owning a car vs. using the services of companies providing passenger transport, *Procedia Computer Science*, vol. 246, 5205–5213.

Jóźwiak Z. (2011), *Problematyka transportu ładunków ponadnormatywnych żeglugą śródlądową*, *Logistyka*, no. 6, 4727–4735.

Jóźwiak Z. (2015), *Ekoinowacje w transporcie i logistyce*, Przegląd Komunalny. Dodatek: Jesteś kreatorem?, *Zostań ekoinnowatorem*, no. 6, 1–23, 1–7.

Kacperczyk R. (2009), *Transport i spedycja*, Warszawa: Difin.

Kamiński M., Pospolita W., Cholewiński M., Łagocka A. (2016), *Emisja zanieczyszczeń z sektora transportu lotniczego i jej wpływ na zdrowie człowieka*, Kosmos. *Problemy Nauk Biologicznych*, vol. 65, no. 4, 487–493.

Kancelaria Sejmu (2007), *Załącznik do obwieszczenia Marszałka Sejmu Rzeczpospolitej Polskiej z dnia 25 stycznia 2007 r. w sprawie ogłoszenia jednolitego tekstu ustawy o drogach publicznych*, Ustawa z dnia 21 marca 1985 r. o drogach publicznych. Dz. U. z 2007 r. Nr 19, poz. 115. Rozdz. I, art. 4.

Kautsch A. (2018), *Organizacja transportu oraz obsługa klientów i kontrahentów. Część 1*, Warszawa: Wydawnictwa Komunikacji i Łączności.

KLM Royal Dutch Airlines. (2025), *SAF: alternatywne paliwo lotnicze*: www.klm.pl/information/sustainability/saf.

Kniaziewicz T. (2024), *Ekologia w transporcie wodnym*, Dąbrowa Górnicza: Polskie forum transportu, logistyki i spedycji, 27–28 czerwiec 2024 r.

Kolejowa Strona Przepisowa (2025), Instrukcja R-60 o technologii pracy stacji manewrowej: http://kolej.krb.com.pl/r60/rozdz1.html.

Konieczna I. (2024), Co to jest transport całopojazdowy?: https://prilo.com/pl/co-to-jest-transport-calopojazdowy/

Kowalska G., Hawlena J., Rowiński R. (2023), *Determinants of air transport development*, *European Research Studies Journal*, vol. XXVI, no. 1, 108–120.

Koźlak A. (2018), *Inteligentne systemy jako instrument poprawy efektywności transportu*, *Logistyka*, no. 2, 369–379.

Kraśkiewicz A., Oleksiewicz W., Lipko C. (2016), *Terminologia i systematyka elementów składowych w nawierzchni kolejowej o konstrukcji bezpodsypkowej*, Zeszyty Naukowo-Techniczne Stowarzyszenia Inżynierów i Techników Komunikacji Rzeczpospolitej Polskiej, *Oddział w Krakowie*, vol. 2, no. 109, 101–114.

Kujda P., Pawlak K. (2020), *Ekologiczne rozwiązania zrównoważonego transportu publicznego – niskoemisyjność i bezemisyjność środków komunikacji miejskiej*, *Journal of Translogistics*, vol. 6, no. 1, 67–78.

Liwiński J. (2025), *Długoterminowe prognozy rynku lotniczego Boeinga*: https://zbiam.pl/artykuly/dlugoterminowe-prognozy-rynku-lotniczego-boeinga/.

Majka A. (2024), *Ekologia w transporcie lotniczym*, Dąbrowa Górnicza: Polskie forum transportu, logistyki i spedycji, 27–28 czerwiec 2024 r.

Marczak M. (2014), *Budowa inteligentnych systemów transportowych jako szansa dla zrównoważonego rozwoju regionów*, *Ekonomia i Zarządzanie*, vol. 6, no. 2, 34–42.

Mazurek P. (2010), *Algorytmy superrozdzielczości w inteligentnych systemach inteligentnych systemach transportowych do śledzenia odległych pojazdów*, *Logistyka*, no. 188, 255–262.

MediaLogistyka. Portal, czasopismo, podcast: www.logistyka.net.pl/bank-wiedzy/item/95398-rynek-logistyczny-na-swiecie-ponownie-rosnie-we-wszystkich-obszarach.

Mendyk E. (2009), *Ekonomika transport*, Poznań: Wyższa Szkoła Logistyki.

Merkisz J. (2024), *Ekologia w transporcie*, Dąbrowa Górnicza: Polskie forum transportu, logistyki i spedycji, 27–28 czerwiec 2024.

Michalski E. (2024), *Marketing. Podręcznik akademicki*, Warszawa: PWN.

Mwaniki P. (2025), *Top 10 largest airports in North America by land area*: https://constructionreviewonline.com/biggest-projects/top-10-largest-airports-in-north-america-by-land-area/?utm_source=chatgpt.com.

Nahum A. (1996), *Maszyny latające*, Warszawa: Arkady.

Nakolei.pl website, *Polska superszybka kolej magnetyczna na tradycyjnych torach*: www.nakolei.pl/polska-superszybka-kolej-magnetyczna-na-tradycyjnych-torach/.

Neider J. (2006), *Transport w handlu międzynarodowym*, Gdańsk: Wydawnictwo Uniwersytetu Gdańskiego.

Neider J. (2015), *Transport międzynarodowy*, Warszawa: PWE.

Nowosielski T. (2008), *Infrastrukturalne uwarunkowania rozwoju logistyki morskiej*, [in:] *Funkcjonowanie systemów logistycznych*, Jaworski J., Mytlewski A. (eds.), Warszawa: Wyższa Szkoła Bankowa w Gdańsku.

Official website of General Directorate for National Roads and Motorways: www.gov.pl/web/gddkia/znaki-zmiennej-tresci---tak-samo-wazne-jak-tradycyjne.

Oflakowski K. (2024), *Rynek logistyczny na świecie ponownie rośnie we wszystkich obszarach*: https://logistyka.rp.pl/produkty-i-uslugi/art41097931-rynek-logistyczny-na-swiecie-ponownie-rosnie.

Orczyk M. (2024), *Hałas w transporcie*, Dąbrowa Górnicza: Polskie forum transportu, logistyki i spedycji, 27–28 czerwiec 2024 r.

Pabian A., Pabian B., Bilińska K. (2025), Proposal of a model for improving the management of the wind energy industry in the context of sustainable development challenges, *Energies*, vol. 18, no. 4, 1–15.

PESA. (2025), Homepage: https://pesa.pl/produkty/lokomotywy/gama-dualpower-111-de/.

Pielecha I. (2024), *Ekologia w transporcie drogowym*, Dąbrowa Górnicza: Polskie forum transportu, logistyki i spedycji, 27–28 czerwiec 2024 r.

Portal Kolejowy (2025), *PKP PLK testują nową nawierzchnie kolejową*. https://kolejowyportal.pl/pkp-plk-testuja-nowa-nawierzchnie-kolejowa-cichsza-i-trwalsza/.

Rabe M. (2019), *Rozwój i konkurencyjność transportu towarów koleją w Polsce*, *Ekonomika i Organizacja Logistyki*, vol. 4, no.2, 81–88.

Rothman H. (2001), *50 firm, które zmieniły świat*, Warsaw: Wydawnictwo Amber, .

Ruciński A. (2007), *Transport lotniczy,* [in:] *Transport*, Rydzkowski W., Wojewódzka-Król K. (eds.), PWN: Warszawa 2007.

SCANIA Poland. (2025), www.scania.com/pl/pl/home/about-scania/newsroom/news/2023/scania-super-z-najnizszym-spalaniem-w-european-truck-challenge.html.

Scheibler A., Puchała M. (2021), *Znaczenie rozwoju technologii dla konkurencyjności pasażerskiego transportu lotniczego*, *Zarządzanie Innowacyjne w Gospodarce i Biznesie*, vol. 2, no. 33, 105–127.

Skowron-Grabowska B. (2007), *Place of logistics centres in supply chains in the context of electronic markets*, [in:] *Advanced logistic systems. Theory and practice*, Illes B., Kot S., Telek P. (eds.), Miskolc: University of Miskolc.

Health Effects Institute. (2024), *State of Global Air 2024. Special report. A special report on global exposure to air pollution and its health impacts, with a focus on children's health*, Boston: HEI, IHME.

SEALAND Group. (2025), Ekologiczne rozwiązania morskie –czyli statki z mniejszą ilością CO2: www.sealand.com.pl/pl/baza-wiedzy/nowe-technologie-morskie.

Sussman J. (2000), *Introduction to transportation systems*, Boston: Artech House.

Sysak J. (1982), *Drogi kolejowe,* Warszawa: PWN.

Szałucki K. (2007), *Transport samochodowy,* [in:] *Transport,* Rydzkowski W., Wojewódzka-Król K. (eds.), Warszawa: PWN.

Szwankowski S. (2017), *Transport samochodowy,* [in:] *Transport,* Rydzkowski W., Wojewódzka-Król K. (eds.), Warszawa: PWN.

Towpik K. (2009), *Infrastruktura transportu kolejowego*, Warszawa: Oficyna Wydawnicza Politechniki Warszawskiej.

Urbanyi-Popiołek I. (2013), *Ekonomiczne i organizacyjne aspekty transportu*, Bydgoszcz: Wydawnictwo Uczelniane Wyższej Szkoły Gospodarki w Bydgoszczy.

Urząd Transportu Kolejowego (2025), *Eko kolej*: https://dane.utk.gov.pl/sts/eko-kolej.

Witkowski K (2016), *Problematyka zanieczyszczenia atmosfery przez statki wykorzystywane w transporcie morskim*, *Bezpieczeństwo i Ekologia*, vol. 17, no. 6, 468–473.

Wiktorowska-Jasik A. (2016), *Rozwój transportu drogowego w ujęciu historycznym – najważniejsze osiągnięcia światowej motoryzacji*, *Transport, Logistyka, Porty*, no. 1, 15–19.

Włudyka S, Orłowski K. (2009), *Ecological aspects of logistics in various kinds of transport*, *Scientific Journals. Maritime University of Szczecin*, vol. 16, no. 88, 270–275.

Wojciechowski Ł., Wojciechowski A., Kosmatka T. (2009), *Infrastruktura magazynowa i transportowa*, Poznań: Wyższa Szkoła Logistyki.

Wojewódzka – Król K. (2007), *Infrastruktura transportu*, [in:] *Usługi logistyczne*, Rydzkowski W. (eds.), Poznań: Biblioteka Logistyka.

Wojewódzka-Król K. (2008), *Infrastruktura transportu wodnego śródlądowego*, [in:] *Transport*, Rydzkowski W., Wojewódzka – Król K. (eds.), Warszawa: PWN.

Wyraz E. (2016), *Efektywność transportu wodnego śródlądowego i lotniczego*, *Autobusy*, vol. 17, no. 6, 714–717.

Żak J. (2009) *Transport*, [in:] *Logistyka*, Kisperska – Moroń D., Krzyżaniak S. (eds.), Poznań: Biblioteka Logistyka.

Zalewski P., Siedlecki P., Drewnowski A. (2014), *Technologia transportu kolejowego*, Warszawa: Wydawnictwa Komunikacji i Łączności.

Zrównoważone nie zrównoważone. (2025), www.easa.europa.eu/pl/light/topics/european-aviation-environmental-report-2025.

3

Telematics Systems in Road Transport Companies

Classification, Functionality and Role in Managing Transport Operations

3.1 General Characteristics of Telematics Systems

Telematics systems, as a key component of modern information infrastructures, are playing an increasingly important role in management and steering processes in complex technological environments. Their applications now extend beyond the traditionally understood field of communication, encompassing both automatic data processing and dynamic, real-time analysis. Nowadays, telematics is not only a technological field, but also an important tool for the transformation of socio-economic processes. This chapter aims to present a general overview of telematics systems with particular emphasis on their definitions, components, functional properties, and application potential. Modern telematics systems constitute a key element of society's information infrastructure, integrating telecommunications, IT, and automation technologies to effectively transmit, process, and analyse data. Their dynamic development is accompanied by widespread application – in numerous economic sectors, such as energy, healthcare, crisis management and, above all, in logistics and transportation. A fundamental feature of telematics systems is their ability to connect distributed information sources in real time, enabling quick, and accurate decisions based on current data. The development of telematics systems in Europe was a consequence of the integration

DOI: 10.1201/9781003646518-4

of the European Union's transport policy with modern technological solutions.

The concept of telematics has gained importance because of the dynamic development of modern information and communication technologies, and its practical application has gradually expanded to various areas of life and the economy. The term itself originates from the French language (*télématique*) and is a combination of two words: *télécommunication* (telecommunication) and *informatique* (informatics). Firstly, it appeared in an official report prepared in 1978 by S. Nora and A. Minc for the French government. By the 1980s, the term started to be also widely used in the English language as telematics (Mikulski, 2010, pp. 36–37).

Telematics is an interdisciplinary field that deals with the integration of information technology, telecommunications, and automation. Its primary function is to support the operation of physical systems by collecting, processing, and transmitting information tailored to the needs of a given operating environment. Telematics is a relatively young, but at the same time, dynamically developing field of knowledge, developed in response to the rapid development of communication and information technologies. Its origins are related to the need to integrate information technology, telecommunications, and control systems within modern decision support and information management systems. This term, initially used in specialist circles, penetrated into general language over time, with its meaning and scope of applications gradually evolving. Telematics is therefore integrated telecommunications, IT, and information solutions, often supported by elements of automatic control whose functionality is adapted to serve physical systems efficiently. These are spatially distributed systems that perform specific tasks, taking into account infrastructure environmental, and organizational conditions as well as the requirements of users and operators. A characteristic feature of telematics is its flexibility in terms of applications.

To sum up the above, telematics is a combination of two concepts: telecommunications and computer science, the meanings of which precisely reflect the scope of applications of this interdisciplinary area of knowledge. Telecommunications refers to technologies that enable the transfer of information over distance between a sender and a recipient. Etymologically, it is derived from the Greek prefix *tele*, meaning "far," and the Latin verb *communicare*, translated as "to share" or "to communicate". Informatics (computer science), in turn, covers theoretical and practical aspects of information processing from algorithmizing, through data storage, to their effective transmission and analysis in computer systems. Therefore, the term being characterized is usually accompanied by an adjective indicating the field of application, e.g. transport telematics, medical telematics, city telematics, or library telematics. The concept of telematics, which is the result of the integration of the fields of telecommunications and computer science, is characterized by complexity that can be precisely defined by distinguishing four basic functional components. Each of these components reflects a separate structural or operational dimension, and their mutual complementarity determines the coherence and effectiveness of the telematics systems' functioning as a whole. This approach allows for a comprehensive approach to telematics as an integrated system for collecting, processing and transmitting information in the context of communication and data management. The highlighted components are (Table 3.1): internal communication, remote information transmission, information management and automation.

The analysis of the four fundamental dimensions of communication, transmission of information, information management as well as automation allows to define telematics as an integrated technological system whose essence is intelligent information management in environments that are both spatially and functionally distributed. Telematics systems, as multi-faceted cyber-physical systems, enable continuous exchange, processing, and distribution of data to support decision-making processes, optimize operations, and ensure smooth information flow in complex environments.

In the light of the previously discussed definitions of telecommunications and IT, the term "telematics" can be precisely defined as a set of systems and processes aimed at remote data exchange, their automatic processing, storage, and making available in a form that is adapted to the diverse needs of users. A telematics system is an organized technological structure that integrates both hardware components (terminal devices, sensors, communication

Table 3.1 Fundamental Components of Telematics Systems

INTERNAL COMMUNICATION	Internal communication, defined as the process of data exchange between individual system components, encompasses both interactions between peripheral devices and data transmission between local components and the central system. In this context, telematics systems must demonstrate the ability to ensure the continuity, integrity, and consistency of real-time information flow, both unidirectionally (e.g. monitoring functions) and bidirectionally (e.g. remote control and management).
REMOTE INFORMATION TRANSMISSION	Remote transmission of information using modern, commonly used telecommunications technologies. These solutions enable the efficient transfer of data from endpoint devices to central management systems, often in the context of high mobility of users and devices. Wireless communication technologies such as GSM, LTE, and 5G are particularly important in this regard, providing essential system flexibility and enabling their efficient operation in conditions of a dynamically changing environment.
INFORMATION MANAGEMENT	A complex and multi-stage process encompassing a number of activities: from data generation (e.g. by on-board sensors), through data acquisition (data collection), storage (in database systems and temporary memories), transmission (transmission in digital form), processing (including logical and analytical operations), up to sharing (e.g. in the form of reports or visualizations). An important element of this process is also the interpretation of information, consisting in adapting its content to the user's perception and needs, which allows the use of data as a basis for undertaking both operational and strategic decisions.
AUTOMATIZATION	It ensures the autonomous operation of telematics systems. It encompasses the processes of data acquisition, analysis and recording in a continuous and independent manner, eliminating the need for constant human intervention. This solution enables immediate sharing of information with the end user or automatic transfer of data to subsequent layers of the system – including decision-making, control, or analytical systems – for further processing and actions.

Source: Own elaboration.

modules) as well as software elements (data processing systems, analytical algorithms, user interfaces) whose primary function is to acquire information from the environment, transmit it remotely using ICT technologies, and then interpret, analyse and present it – often in real or near-real mode.

A key feature of telematics systems is the ability to dynamically adapt the content and form of data to the current operational context and end-user requirements. Thanks to the usage of advanced communication technologies, such as wireless systems (GSM, LTE, 5G), cloud architectures, artificial intelligence (AI) algorithms and edge computing mechanisms, telematics systems play a fundamental role in modern environments that are distributed both functionally and geographically. They constitute the basis for decision support tools, for optimization of operational processes, as well as the development of intelligent management systems, enabling the smooth and secure flow of information in complex structures (Österle, Winter, 2003, p. 55). Telematics systems have a number of common functional properties, as shown in the Figure 3.1.

The most crucial aspect of telematics is information processing: its acquisition, transmission, transformation, distribution, and use in decision-making processes. Telematics systems can operate

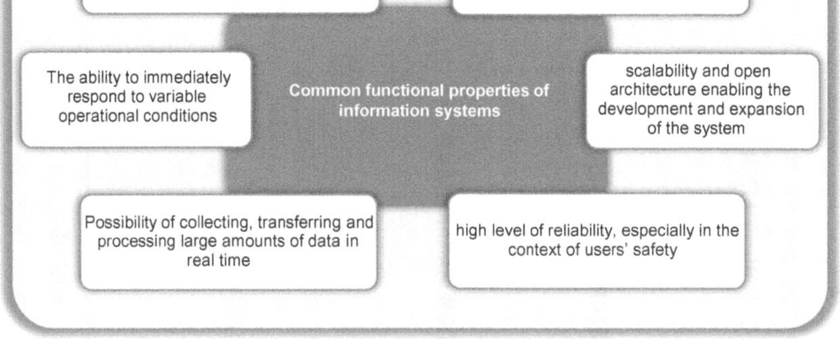

Figure 3.1 Common functional properties of information systems.

Source: Own elaboration.

based on programmed automatic algorithms or dynamically respond to the actions of operators, dispatchers, or end users. An important feature of these systems is their ability to coordinate the work of various subsystems within a single coherent structure.

Telematics solutions are therefore the foundation of so-called smart systems, which can cover various scales – from individual objects, such as smart buildings, to extensive infrastructure systems, such as smart cities or global communication networks. Their complexity is not determined solely by the spatial scope, but mainly by the amount and variety of data and the complexity of the processes being processed. Thanks to their ability to integrate various devices and functions, telematics systems are used in many areas, such as transport, medicine, finance, city management, and digital.[1] Modern telematics systems are characterized by several key functional features. These include: the ability to respond immediately to changing operating conditions, the ability to process large data sets in real time, flexibility in integrating various technological elements, what is more – reliability, which translates into user safety. An important aspect of these systems is also their scalability, which allows their gradual expansion depending on the user's needs[3]. From the point of view of technical structure, telematics systems consist of a set of devices and applications responsible for various stages of information processing – from data acquisition, through their analysis, to the presentation of results to the end user. Telematics systems use a variety of technical components (Figure 3.2).

These systems are designed to operate in real time, using efficient databases and standard communication interfaces. They are required to be highly reliable and capable of further integration of new functionalities (Wydro, 2005, pp. 116–130). Telematics systems are therefore understood as sets of solutions combining information, communication and automation technologies, designed to meet the needs of physical systems – from linear infrastructure to vehicles and transport systems' operators.[2] Due to the high variability of operating environments and the dynamic development of digital technologies, telematics systems are characterized by a high degree of modularity and openness, which allows them to be adapted to the diverse needs of users.

Telematics systems, as complex technological structures, are a key element of modern information infrastructures, enabling data

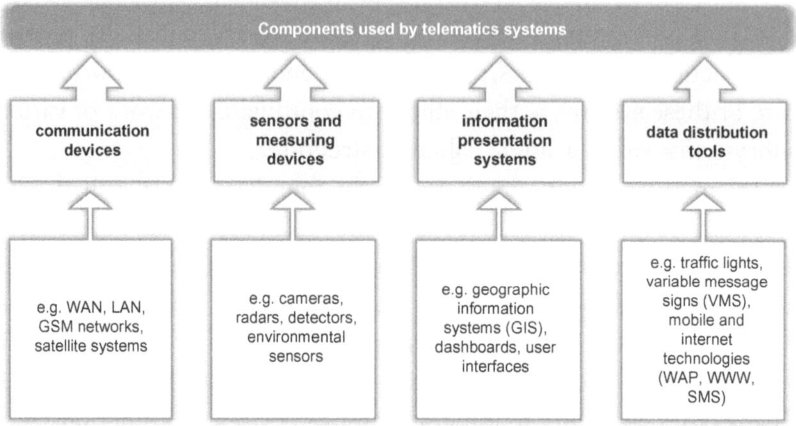

Figure 3.2 Components used by telematics systems.

Source: Own elaboration.

management in environments with a high degree of spatial and functional dispersion. Telematics, the result of the integration of telecommunications, information technology, and automation is a dynamic field of growing importance in the context of global digital transformation. Its essence lies not only in enabling information exchange but, above all, in intelligent data processing, contextualization, and adaptation to the operational, and decision-making needs of end users. The key conclusion from the analysis of telematics systems is their nature as cyber-physical systems in which various technological and functional components interact – from peripheral devices, through communication networks, to analytical layers. These systems not only respond to the growing demands for real-time information processing, but also create the conditions for designing scalable, flexible solutions that can be adapted to the changing needs of economic and social sectors. The development of telematics is evolutionary in nature, closely related to technological progress, standardization of communication solutions and integration with modern data processing methods, including AI algorithms and edge computing. As a result, telematics systems are becoming the foundation of modern infrastructure management strategies, process optimization, and increasing safety and operational efficiency in complex, dynamic, and context-sensitive environments.

3.2 Modern Telematics Solutions for Fleet Management in Road Transport

The development of telematics systems used in road transport companies has been closely linked to advances in telecommunications technologies. Telematics systems used in transport companies can be classified according to a number of technical, organizational, and functional criteria that define their architecture, operation, and scope of application. Key classification aspects include (Figure 3.3).

Due to the wide range of available solutions, telematics systems are now a key element of information infrastructure in road transport

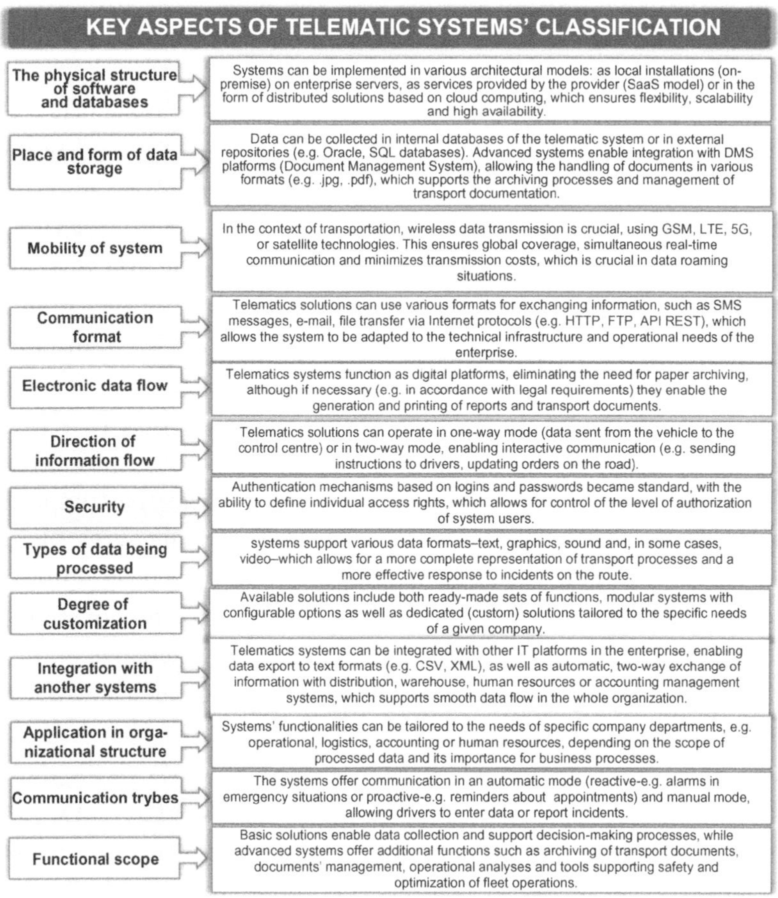

Figure 3.3 Key aspects of the classification of telematics systems in transport companies.

Source: Own elaboration.

companies. Their diversity in terms of architecture, functions, and integration capabilities allows the system to be precisely tailored to the needs of a specific organization. At the same time, the complexity of the market offer poses a challenge in terms of selecting the optimal solution that would best suit the specific nature of a given company's operations and its strategic goals. Modern telematics systems used in road transport cover a wide range of functions and services, integrating technologies for safety, diagnostics, navigation, communication, entertainment, and mobile commerce processes' handling. The foundation for implementing these complex services is data transmission, which provides remote access to information, enables two-way communication between the vehicle and the user, and integration with external infrastructure such as traffic management systems, logistics platforms, and road toll collection devices.

In the context of car road transport, telematics systems play a key role due to their ability to automatically acquire, process, archive, and present operational data. This becomes particularly important in the case of transport companies that carry out transport over long distances, often in different legal jurisdictions and operating conditions. In such environments, access to current information on vehicles' location, technical condition, parameters of transported loads, and drivers' working hours in real time is crucial to ensure efficiency, safety and compliance with legal regulations. It is worth noting that the potential of telematics systems increases proportionally to the scale of road transport operations, where the complexity of logistics operations, the number of vehicles being serviced, and the amount of data processed require the use of advanced information technologies. Telematics is therefore becoming a tool of strategic importance, enabling the rapid, precise and secure exchange of information between a company's central systems and on-board devices installed in vehicles. Information obtained from peripheral devices, such as Global Positioning System (GPS) modules, tachographs, operating parameter sensors, and temperature recorders – are automatically filtered, processed and integrated in central systems, and then distributed to end users in the appropriate form and time which is adapted to specific operational roles (e.g. dispatchers, fleet managers, analysts, and so on). Telematics systems are therefore an integral part of the ecosystem of tools supporting road transport management, including, among others (Figure 3.4).

Modern transport telematics is therefore the foundation of modern, integrated management of logistics processes, enabling data-based decision-making in real time and effective optimization of operations in a dynamic transport environment (Figure 3.5).

The collection and processing of data from a growing number of sources, as well as their integration with other systems operating in a transport company, have opened up new perspectives for the development of telematics systems. Thanks to their extensive data architecture, these systems are transforming from monitoring tools into complex platforms that support decision-making processes in fleet management and transport order fulfilment. Access to detailed, up-to-date, and high-quality data from current transport operations enables immediate response to situational changes – such as delays, random

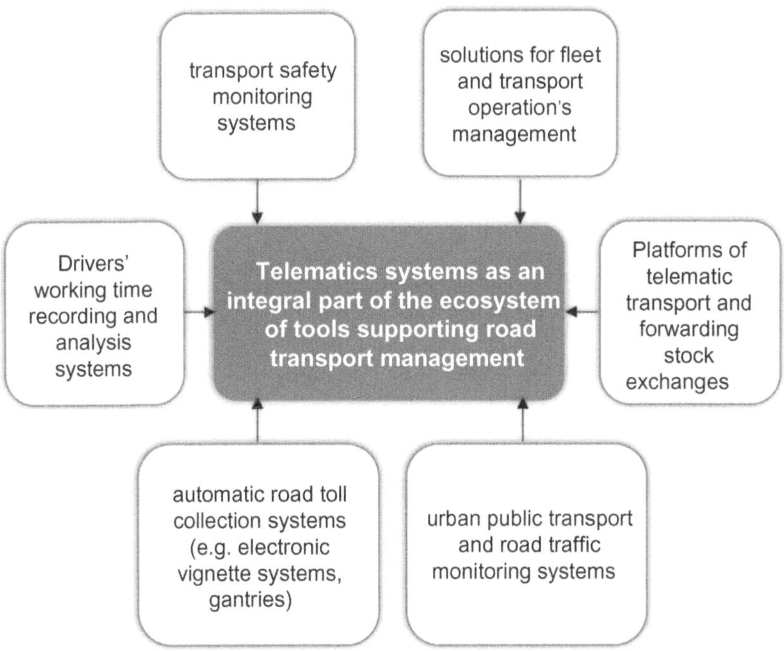

Figure 3.4 Telematics systems as an integral part of the ecosystem of tools supporting road transport management.

Source: Own elaboration.

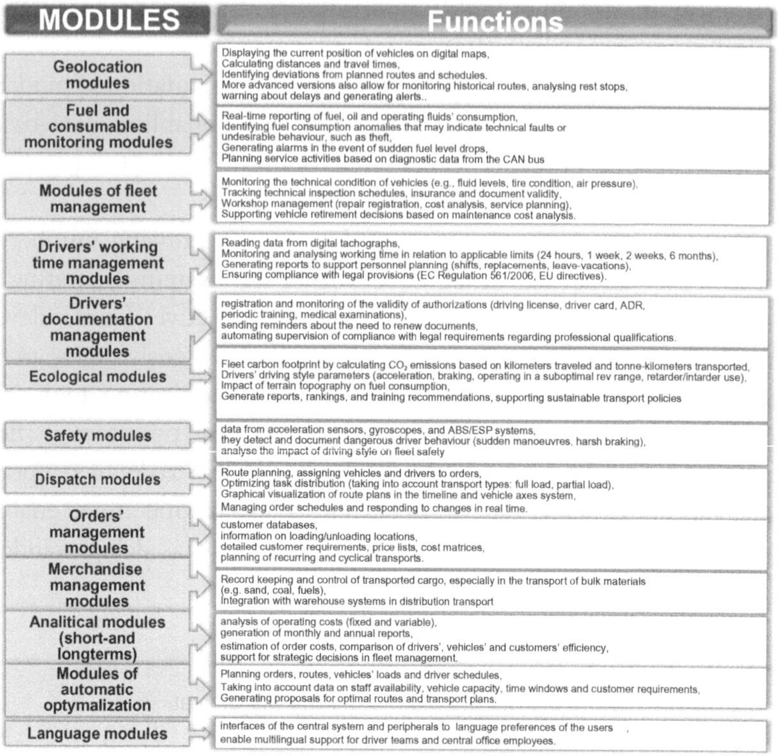

Figure 3.5 Modules and functions of nowadays telematic systems.

Source: Own elaboration.

events, or changes in road conditions – which can be reported to the central system in real time. This information can be immediately used to dynamically adjust schedules, route plans, or operational decisions. Functional modules of telematics systems can operate as standalone components, cooperate with each other within an integrated ecosystem as well as exchange data with other enterprise management systems, such as:

- ERP systems (Enterprise Resource Planning),
- TMS systems (Transport Management System),
- WMS systems (Warehouse Management System),
- CRM systems (Customer Relationship Management),
- dedicated analytical applications (Business Intelligence, BI).

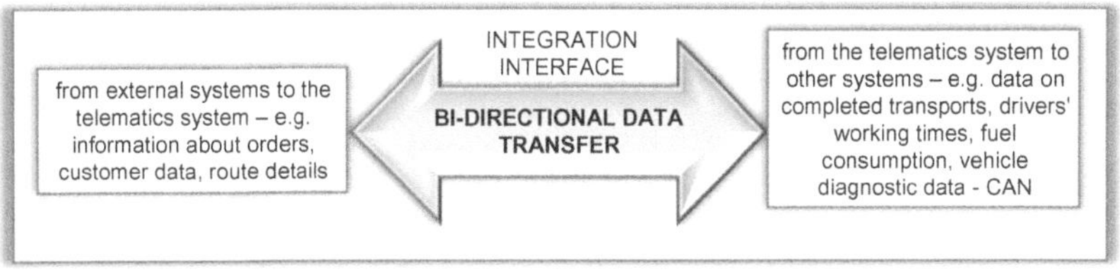

Figure 3.6 Bidirectional data transfer with the usage of the integration interface.

Source: Own elaboration.

Thanks to integration interfaces provided by telematics system manufacturers, bidirectional data transfer is possible (Figure 3.6).

Such an integration significantly reduces the time needed for information to circulate within the company, enabling a more efficient completion of the transport process after the shipment has been carried out and eliminating the need to repeatedly enter the same data manually into different systems – which significantly reduces the risk of human error, improves data quality, and increases the efficiency of operational processes. Implementing communication between telematics systems and other IT systems in a transport company requires defining appropriate data exchange interfaces (np. API REST, SOAP, CSV/XML/JSON files) as well as defining the communication mode and protocol (HTTP/HTTPS, MQTT, WebSocket, FTP/SFTP). This process usually involves integration work on the part of system providers, who must adapt solutions to the specific needs of the company, creating a consistent and reliable data exchange channel. The key role of telematics solutions is the acquisition of data regarding the location of vehicles, carried out using devices installed in fleet vehicles.[3] In the case of more advanced systems, it is also possible to transmit data from the central system to peripheral devices located in vehicles. These systems use geolocation technology based on the integration of communication modules with the function of localization and GPS modules (a device that receives signals from the GPS satellites to determine the geographic location of the device) – all together, dedicated to satellite navigation. The communication module, which uses data obtained directly from the cellular network infrastructure, enables determining the device's location by analysing information about the base stations to which the mobile device is connected, as illustrated in Figure 3.7.

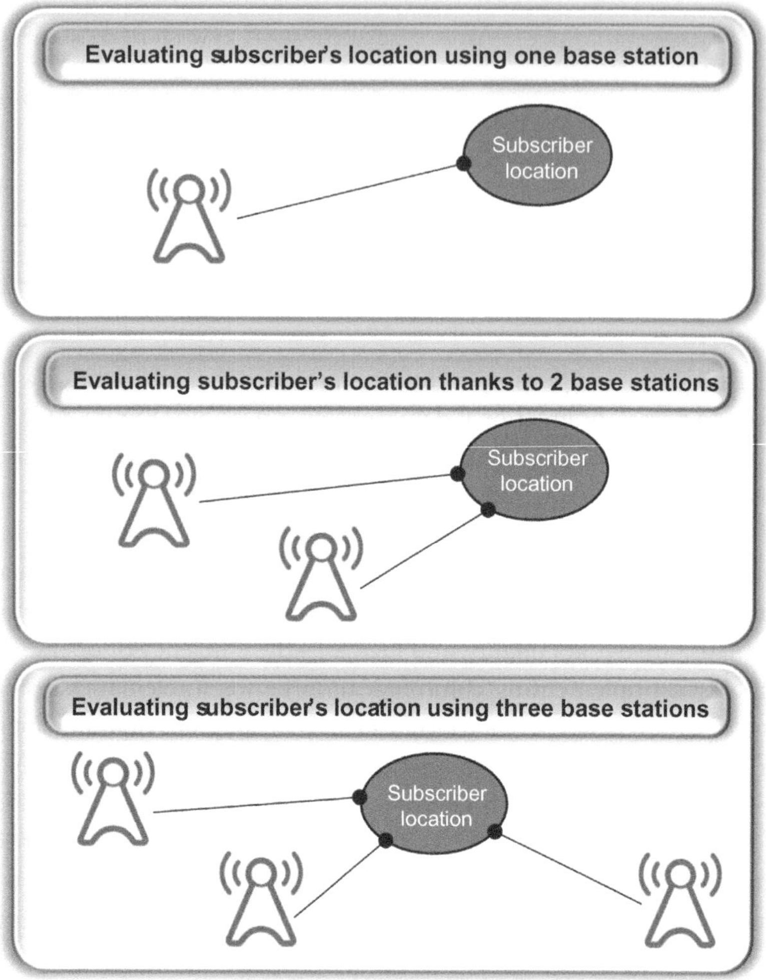

Figure 3.7 Techniques for determining the user's location based on information from a network of base stations.

Source: Own elaboration.

The accuracy of the location depends on the number of base stations with which the connection is currently established, as well as on the technologies used by the system to calculate the location based on data from the cellular network. In urban areas with a high density of base stations, it is even possible to achieve location accuracy of 50 metres.[4]

GPS modules are a commonly used solution in telematics systems, especially for geolocation functions, due to their ability to provide high-precision positioning regardless of the degree of urbanization of the area. GPS technology is based on the analysis of signals transmitted by a constellation of satellites, which enable the calculation of the distance between the receiving device and individual satellites. This process uses the Time Difference of Arrival (TDoA) method of analysing the time differences in the reception of the signal to determine the geographical coordinates of the receiver. To determine a position, it is necessary to receive signals from at least three satellites, although in practice, a larger number of available satellites translates into increased location accuracy. It is worth adding that the precision of geolocation in GPS systems can be additionally supported by differential techniques (DGPS – involves using a base station with known coordinates to correct errors in GPS signals. The base station calculates and transmits correction data to the mobile receiver, which is taken into account in real time or during data processing to improve location accuracy) or augmentation systems such as SBAS (Satellite-Based Augmentation Systems), which allow for further reduction of positioning errors, especially important in critical transport applications. Functionality of telematics systems can be implemented using a variety of mobile device configurations, tailored to the needs of specific applications. In their simplest form, the system consists of a peripheral device equipped with a communication module, a location module, a set of internal sensors, and, if necessary, interfaces enabling the reception of external signals. The whole works in conjunction with a central system responsible for data collection, processing, and visualization. The central system can be located either within the enterprise infrastructure or in external data centres, depending on the implementation model (on-premises or in the cloud). A key element in the architecture of telematics systems is the ability to transmit data wirelessly, which is the basis for their operation. For this purpose, mobile communication technologies are commonly used, such as cellular networks (GSM, UMTS, LTE, 5G), satellite communications, as well as local networks based on the Wi-Fi standard, which in some cases enable data transmission without the need to use paid services of telecommunications operators. The use of wireless communication technologies significantly increases the flexibility and range of telematics systems, which is particularly important in the context of fleet management in road transport. Progress in the development of cellular network technology, including the transition from 2G (GSM) standards to newer generations such as 3G (UMTS), 4G (LTE), and 5G, has significantly expanded the possibilities of data transmission from peripheral devices to central management systems. Increased throughput and reduced data transmission latency enable transmission over shorter time intervals, enabling near-instantaneous transmission of telemetry data such as vehicle position, technical parameters, and operational status. High availability of transmission bands in cellular networks, multiple access modulation techniques (e.g. OFDMA in LTE, 5G), and the use of transmission quality control mechanisms (QoS) enable reliable and efficient data transfer from peripheral devices to central systems. Thanks to this, telematics systems can constantly update information on the fleet status, support real-time analyses and enable operational decisions based on current data, which is particularly important in the dynamic road transport environment.

The first generations of telematics systems used text messaging technology (SMS) as the primary communication channel between peripheral devices installed in vehicles and the central management system. Data transmission could be initiated in two ways: by sending an SMS message from the central system containing a specific code that triggered a response with information about the vehicle's location, or by setting fixed time intervals in which the peripheral device sent data to the central system. SMS-based solutions were used at a time when cellular network standards did not yet support packet data transmission. This changed with the introduction of GPRS (General Packet Radio Service) technology in 2000, which enabled packet data transmission similar to that used in computer networks. Thanks to the use of GPRS, it became possible to transmit data in a more flexible and efficient way – users could use both SMS transmission and the transmission of data packets, which were divided into smaller units and transmitted via shared channels of the cellular network. GPRS technology enabled throughputs of 30–80 kbit/s, which, compared to previous solutions based solely on SMS, represented a significant step forward in the development of transport telematics. This enabled more effective monitoring of vehicle location and the transmission of a wider range of diagnostic data, contributing to the increased functionality of telematics systems in road transport. The introduction of subsequent generations of data transmission technologies, such as EDGE (Enhanced Data rates for GSM Evolution – enabling transmission of up to 236 kbit/s), UMTS (Universal Mobile Telecommunications System – up to 384 kbit/s), HSDPA (High Speed Downlink Packet Access – download speed up to 14.4 Mbit/s), HSUPA (High Speed Uplink Packet Access – upload speed up to 5.76 Mbit/s), HSPA, and HSPA+ (download up to 21.6 Mbit/s and upload up to 5.76 Mbit/s, respectively), as well as LTE (Long Term Evolution – enabling data download speeds up to 150 Mbit/s and upload speeds up to 50 Mbit/s), was a breakthrough in the development of mobile technologies. In a historical perspective, the increase in data transmission speed between the first generations of network technologies and modern solutions can be expressed as a 3000-fold increase in throughput of downloaded data and a 1666-fold increase in the speed of outgoing data transmission.

For telematics systems, such technological advancements translate into fundamental changes in the way communication is implemented. It has become possible not only to significantly shorten data transmission intervals but also to implement communication in a nearly continuous mode, enabling the ongoing exchange of information between peripheral devices and the central system. Furthermore, the increase in available bandwidth allows for the transmission of significantly larger volumes of data, including detailed diagnostic information, multimedia data, and complex telemetry packets. At the same time, significant reductions in data transmission costs are being observed, particularly in data roaming charges. This is a key factor for road transport companies – it enables continuous, geographically independent communication between the vehicle fleet and central systems, at the same time eliminating the need to incur additional costs related to data roaming. This trend promotes the integration of logistics processes on a global scale and increases the efficiency of cross-border transport management. In the early stages of development, telematics systems offered a limited range of functions, mainly focused on the basic usage of location data obtained via GPS technology. The main functionality involved the ability to visualize the vehicle's current position on a map – both at the user's request and within pre-programmed, cyclical time intervals. This was a form of passive monitoring, allowing only basic insight into the vehicle's location.

The functions of telematics systems have been extended, over time, to include the ability to replay and analyse the route travelled at specified time intervals, which enabled the reconstruction of the route for control and optimization purposes. Additionally, mechanisms were introduced to compare the planned route, generated by the navigation system, with the actual route travelled by the vehicle. These analyses included both a visual summary of routes on a digital map and a comparison of parameters such as total distance and travel time. Extensive reporting systems also enabled the identification and visualization of stopover points and their durations as well as the generation of warnings in the event of exceeding permissible time limits or stopping in restricted zones (so-called: geofencing). This information could be presented in the form of reports generated automatically by the central system at predefined time intervals or generated upon user request. The introduction of these features marked a significant step towards automating fleet management and supervision processes, increasing the level of operational control and supporting the optimization of routes and driver working hours.

With technological advances going on, telematics systems have further evolved, going beyond the traditional functions of location monitoring and tracking travel parameters. Currently, telematics solutions integrate advanced technologies such as AI, machine learning (ML), and real-time data analysis (real-time analytics), which allows the automation of fleet management processes as well as predictive modelling of vehicles' and drivers' behaviour. New generation systems enable comprehensive analysis of operational data, including not only the vehicle's position, but also the operating parameters of the drive unit (such as engine speed, fuel consumption, exhaust emission levels), data from safety sensors (e.g. ADAS systems, cameras monitoring the vehicle's surroundings, proximity sensors), as well as environmental data (e.g. weather conditions, road surface quality, traffic density). Integrating this information allows for the creation of advanced optimization models that support operational decisions in route planning, operating cost management, predicting the risk of breakdowns, and assessing drivers' driving style. Another crucial element of telematics systems development is integration with ERP systems, which enables seamless data exchange between modules responsible for fleet management, logistics, accounting, and customer service. This enables the full replication of a company's business processes in a digital environment, significantly streamlining supply chain management and enabling ongoing optimization of operating costs. Modern telematics systems, using cloud computing technologies and microservice architecture, are characterized by high scalability, availability, and the ability to remotely manage the fleet from anywhere in the world. Solutions based on APIs and interoperability standards enable the integration of data from various sources, creating a coherent information ecosystem that can be used for advanced analyses, trend forecasting and data-driven decision-making.

In the case of special transports, including transport carried out using specialized technologies – such as the transport of liquid materials, concrete mixtures, chemicals, or products sensitive to temperature changes – advanced telematics systems offer the possibility of integration with electronic systems monitoring the operation of semi-trailers and trailers. These types of solutions enable bidirectional data exchange between the drive unit and the transport unit, which enables monitoring and automatic reporting of key operational parameters – see Figure 3.8.

Thanks to such functions, telematics systems become a key tool supporting the safety and quality of specialized transport, enabling the optimization of logistics processes as well as meeting regulatory requirements and quality standards in the transport of sensitive materials.

A breakthrough in the development of telematics technologies was the introduction of the possibility of direct access to digital vehicle communication buses, in particular to the CAN-Bus (Controller Area Network) standard. The integration of peripheral devices with the CAN thoroughfare enables the acquisition and transmission of a wide range of vehicle diagnostic and operational data, including information about its current position, to the central telematics system in continuous mode. By using signals from the CAN thoroughfare, it is possible to monitor parameters such as: fuel level in the tank, current gear shift position, accelerator, and brake pedal pressure, vehicle speed as well as many other key diagnostic data, including operating fluid temperature, safety system status, tire condition, and information on

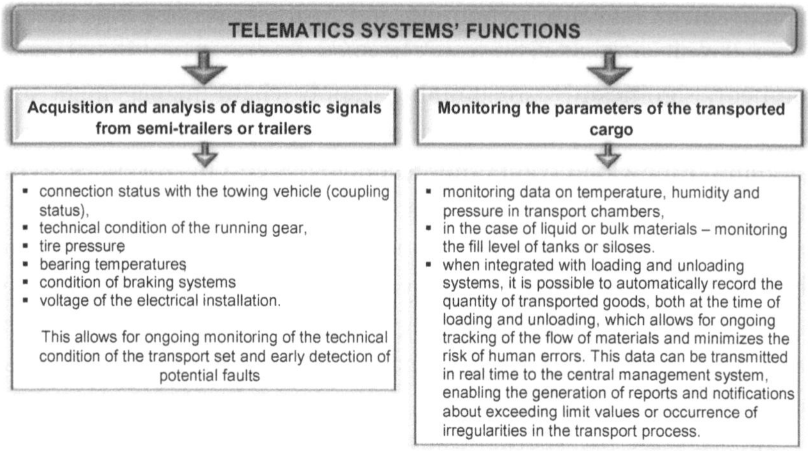

Figure 3.8 Functions of telematic systems.

Source: Own elaboration.

the activation of driver assistance systems. The greatest opportunities for using CAN bus signals are available to truck manufacturers who design integrated telematics systems directly in the vehicle's electronic architecture. In such systems, telemetry data is directly accessible from the vehicle's control units (ECUs), without the need for additional intermediary devices such as external CAN interfaces. This type of integration provides full access to all signals generated by vehicle systems, which is a competitive advantage for manufacturers – they have full knowledge of the data structure, signal formats, and diagnostic capabilities offered by the vehicle. Telematics systems developed by truck manufacturers place particular emphasis on supporting operational efficiency and ecological fleet operation. These include real-time driver assistance functions, eco-driving support, fuel, and consumables monitoring, CO2 emission reporting, driving style analysis and driver and vehicle performance rankings. Thanks to this, these solutions become not only a tool for monitoring the location of vehicles, but also a comprehensive system supporting the optimization of operating costs, improvement of safety, and implementation of sustainable development policies in transport companies.

Another external signal source that can be integrated with telematics system peripherals is the digital tachograph. This device provides key operational data related to driver work, including statuses such as driving, non-driving work, breaks, and availability. This information enables monitoring of transport compliance with labour law and drivers' working time regulations. Additionally, the digital tachograph enables the acquisition of diagnostic data from the vehicle, including information from odometer, which allows for precise monitoring of the distance travelled by the vehicle over a specific period of time. Telematics systems can not only read data from the tachograph in real time, but also send it to the central fleet management system and archive it, which is a legal requirement for transport fleet operators in the European Union, in accordance with Regulation (EC) No. 561/2006 in force since 1 May 2006, and Directive 2002/15/EC on the organization of drivers' working time. Integrating the digital tachograph with telematics systems allows for the automation of the working time data management process, eliminating the need to manually read data from driver cards and tachographs, and also enables the quick generation of reports and analyses, which significantly improves administrative processes in transport companies.

The development of high-bandwidth data transmission technologies, enabling the transfer of large amounts of information in real time, has created the foundation for the implementation of full two-way communication between peripheral devices and the central telematics system. As a result, advanced peripherals equipped with on-screen interfaces have appeared on the market, enabling drivers to actively interact with the system – both by receiving messages from the control centre and initiating feedback. With the introduction of the driver interface, telematics systems have gained new functionalities, allowing for the acquisition of additional operational data directly from the driver. The key application of such a solution is to enable the driver to provide information on current operational statuses – such as the start or completion of loading, unloading, refuelling the vehicle, or reporting the causes of stops (e.g. traffic jam, police check, breakdown, random event). These systems allow for the flexible definition of predefined messages and also provide the ability to enter any text content or add comments to selected reports, which enables more detailed reporting of events on the route. Modern solutions with driver interface often integrate satellite navigation functions, offering similar capabilities to commercial navigation systems – including optimal route planning, taking into account information on road conditions (e.g. traffic jams, detours, roadworks), and warnings about obstacles. Additionally, some peripheral devices allow to keep a digital vehicle logbook, in which the driver is obliged to perform periodic technical inspections – such as checking the condition of tyres, testing the level of operating fluids or look up for the operation of lights. Mandatory confirmation by the driver of the vehicle's readiness for operation is an important element of operational safety systems and is required in many transport organizations as a preventive procedure, introduced for the minimalization of the risk of faults or road incidents. Integration of two-way communication systems with diagnostic and navigation functions significantly increases the efficiency of fleet management, enabling better operational control, shortening the response time to incidents, and increasing the level of safety in road transport.

Modern telematics systems allow for the definition of electronic inspection reports concerning vehicle's technical condition, which include a list of mandatory checkpoints, such as checking the condition of tyres, correct operation of lighting, confirmation of the braking system test, operating fluid levels, and other key safety elements. Each of these points can be confirmed electronically by the driver, which is an integral part of pre-departure procedures and meets the requirements related to documenting the technical condition of the vehicle before it is put into operation.

The next stage of the development of systems enabling data collection with the participation of the driver has been the implementation of the functionality of recording detailed information on the processes of loading and unloading goods as well as collecting data on contractors – senders and recipients. These systems allow for the entry of data such as specification of the transported cargo (type of goods, its properties, transport requirements), number and type of packaging units, details of the location of loading and unloading points as well as additional notes and comments from the customer or warehouse operator. In traditional telematics systems, where data flow is unilateral – i.e. from the peripheral device and the driver to the headquarters – the driver is required to manually enter data for each new loading or unloading, which is associated with repeatable activities and increased workload, especially in the case of carrying out orders for the same customer on different routes. In response to these limitations, the development of telematics systems has focused on implementing solutions enabling full two-way communication between the driver and the central fleet management system. This makes it possible not only to transmit information from the driver to the headquarters, but also to download data, coming from the central system – such as automatic completion of information about the customer, delivery address, cargo parameters, or assigned safety procedures. This system architecture significantly relieves the driver of the need to manually enter data, reduces the risk of errors, shortens the time of handling documentation, and enables faster response to operational changes, thus increasing the efficiency of the entire logistics process. Two-way communication in telematics systems enables not only the transfer of data from peripheral devices to the central system, but also the provision of feedback to the driver, its editing, and then the return of the completed data to the central system. These solutions enable dynamic management of transport processes, including the transmission of orders, operational instructions, and digital documents. More advanced system implementations, when integrating peripheral devices with the trailer's on-board systems, enable remote, manual, or automatic control of logistics processes, for example, initiating unloading by releasing the cargo release lock. In the case of automatic solutions, geofencing and, security systems are used, such as access locks to control cabinets or unloading systems' locks, which prevent unauthorized unloading outside the designated geographical area.

Another important element of telematics systems are so-called "ecological" modules, which analyse data from the CAN (Controller Area Network – vehicle nervous system – a standardized communication system in vehicles that allows electronic control units to exchange information without complex wiring), internal peripheral sensors, and additional sources in order to assess the driver's driving style. Assessment algorithms can be based on defined criteria such as: maintaining speed within recommended ranges, avoiding harsh acceleration, and braking, driving at optimal engine speeds, proper gear usage, and reducing idling. In more advanced systems, these modules also integrate route data, including analysis of driving style compliance with traffic regulations, speed adjustment to terrain conditions (e.g. hills, curves) and compliance with speed limits. The results of analysis can be presented to the driver in real time, together with suggestions for improving driving techniques as well as sent to the central system, where reports, summaries, and eco-driving rankings are generated.

Telematics systems also enable the operational processes of a transport company to be reflected in electronic forms covering the stages of loading, transport, and delivery of goods to the customer. The driver receives assigned forms directly on the peripheral device's screen, and after completing them, the data is automatically transferred to the central system. Some systems also offer route planning and dispatch modules that integrate databases of loading locations, delivery points and customers, allowing for the optimization of logistics processes without the need for external planning tools.

The variety of hardware platforms used in telematics systems stems from the approach adopted by solution providers. Some systems rely on dedicated terminals designed specifically for a given system, while others utilize widely available mobile devices, such as tablets or smartphones, on which telematics software is installed. Solutions based on standard mobile devices allow making usage of additional functions, such as taking photos (e.g. of documentation of the condition of goods during loading and unloading, photos of transport documents, damage to the vehicle or cargo) as well as recording video sequences, which additionally supports the documentation processes and handling of incidents in transport.

In parallel with the development of the functionality of peripheral devices, which enable the collection of increasingly diverse data at an increasing frequency, significant progress is being observed in the capabilities of central systems in telematics architecture. These systems are not only responsible for receiving and processing information from on-board devices, but also serve increasingly as advanced analytical platforms, integrating data from multiple sources, supporting decision-making processes, generating real-time reports, and creating predictive models of transport processes. The dynamic development of central systems is directly supported by the trend of decreasing data transmission costs, both in the context of domestic transfers and roaming services. Reduction in data transmission costs – resulting from technological progress, liberalization of the telecommunications market and implementation of new communication standards (such as LTE, LTE-Advanced, 5G) – significantly increases the economic profitability of systems enabling the collection and processing of large volumes of telemetry data, even in the case of vehicles operating outside the country. As a result, transport companies gain the ability to conduct advanced monitoring of the technical condition of vehicles, transport parameters, drivers' driving style and fleet location on a continuous basis, regardless of the geographical zone in which their vehicles are currently located. The mentioned trend also enables the implementation of telematics systems as strategic fleet management tools that support the optimization of operating costs, route planning, order profitability analysis, and minimizing operational risks in transport.

The development of telematics systems, their gradual specialization, and the increasing diversity of functions reflect the dynamic changes taking place in the road transport technology sector. Currently, the European market offers an extremely wide range of solutions that respond to the complex needs of transport companies that differ in the scale of their operations, fleet structure, and the specificity of the cargo being transported. There are currently over 100 telematics system suppliers operating on the European market, offering several hundred different solutions dedicated to road transport companies. These systems differ in both their modular architecture and the range of available functions – from basic GPS monitoring to advanced modules for fleet management, safety, fuel consumption and operational data analysis. Differences also include the data transmission technologies being used, such as cellular network communication (GSM, UMTS, LTE, 5G), satellite communication as well as integration with data transmission protocols (e.g. CAN, FMS, API REST). A detailed comparison of available solutions along with an analysis of their functionality and technology is presented in the Table 3.2.

In the context of such a wide market offer, it is crucial to understand what technologies and components make up a telematics system, enabling the implementation of its functions in operational practice. From a technical perspective, a vehicle telematics system must be equipped with an integrated set of hardware and software components

Table 3.2 The Biggest and the Most Recognizable Telematics Providers in Europe (as of 2024)

PROVIDER	HEADQUARTER	DESCRIPTION OF ACTIVITY	SCOPE OF SERVICES
Webfleet (Bridgestone)	Netherlands	One of the leaders in the European market, it has approximately 1.3 million active subscriptions.	Fleet management, location, eco-driving, tachograph.
Verizon Connect	USA / UK	A large global player, present in Europe with an offer for large fleets.	Fleet monitoring, reporting, security.
Geotab	Canada	Strongly developing in Europe (partners in Germany, UK, Poland, etc.)	Open API, advanced analytics, EV monitoring.
Trimble Transport & Logistics	Belgium	Present for decades in the logistics and heavy transport segments.	ITS, route planning, fleet, and drivers' management.
Transics (WABCO/ZF)	Belgium	Focused on heavy transport, forwarding and spedition.	Communication with drivers, TMS telematics, tachograph.
Gurtam (Wialon)	Litwa / Belarus	Wialon Platform – operates through a network of integrators throughout Europe.	Universal platform SaaS for M2M and GPS tracking.
Fleet Complete	Canada / Estonia	It offers integrated solutions for small and medium-sized fleets.	Fleet monitoring, mobile devices, HOS, CAN.
Masternaut (Michelin)	France	Focused on fleet efficiency and CO2 emissions reporting.	Fleet management, eco-driving, ERP integration.
AddSecure Smart Transport	Sweden	A dynamically developing supplier in Scandinavia and Western Europe.	Telematics, tachograph, cold store monitoring.
Eurowag Telematics (W.A.G.)	Czech Republic	Solutions for truck fleets – often integrated with road payments.	GPS, e-toll, fuel management, TMS integration.

Source: Own elaboration.

that enable effective monitoring, management, and communication in real time.

From a technical perspective, a vehicle equipped with a telematics system should include an integrated set of hardware and software components enabling real-time monitoring, management, and communication functions – Figure 3.9.

This technical architecture of a vehicle with a telematics system creates a comprehensive platform enabling the collection and processing of operational data, communication with external systems, and ensuring user safety and comfort. The growing demand for access to reliable, current and precise data in the management of operational processes in road transport companies drives the dynamic development of telematics technologies. The observed trend includes not only an increase in the number of available solutions, but also the progressive diversification of systems' types, functional modules and services offered, which allows for precise adaptation of the architecture of telematics systems to the specific

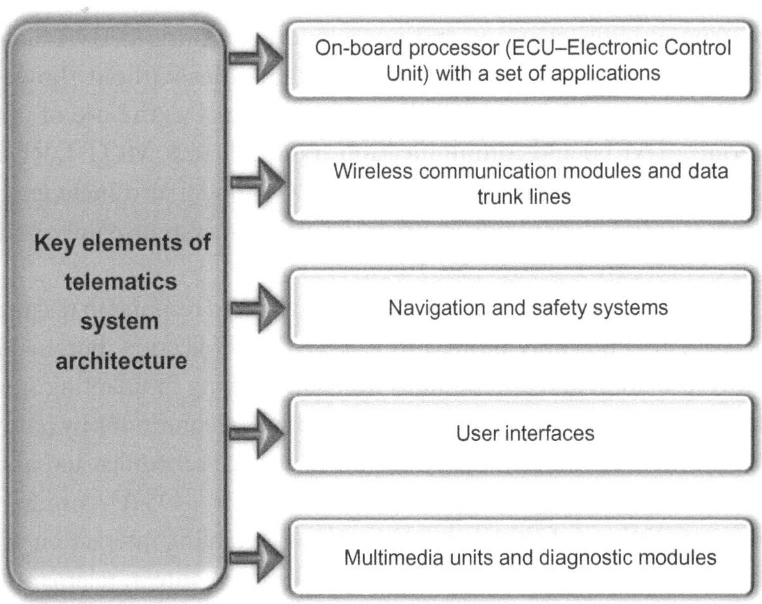

Figure 3.9 Key elements of telematics' system architecture.

Source: Own elaboration.

needs and operational requirements of companies operating in the road transport sector. Modern telematics systems are characterized by a high level of complexity and flexibility, enabling the configuration of extensive information ecosystems that support various areas of enterprise operations – from vehicle monitoring, fleet management, route planning, to the economic analysis of transport operations and the generation of environmental reports. The wide range of functionalities available in modern telematics solutions is a response to the challenges related to the globalization of transport, increasing competition and the need to meet restrictive legal and environmental standards. The future model for road transport telematics systems architecture is defined as the Intelligent Vehicle Network (IVN). The IVN architecture is based on a modular and flexible structure, the central element of which is the Main Control Unit (MCU), which serves as a hub for data processing, information analysis and coordination of system operations. An integral part of the IVN is, so-called: ANA – Adaptive Network Architecture, which enables dynamic exchange of information between vehicle modules, the user and the external infrastructure (e.g. traffic management systems, charging stations, cloud computing). ANA allows for scaling and integration of new functionalities without the need to modify the vehicle's physical structure, thanks to the use of open interfaces (APIs) and communication standards (e.g. MQTT, REST, CAN-XL, Automotive Ethernet). The IVN model also includes the vehicle's internal network, connecting various system components, such as presented in Figure 3.10.

A key feature of IVN is the ability to analyse and respond in real time. The system is not only limited to passive data collection, but enables its interpretation and autonomous decision-making by adapting speed and driving dynamics to road and environmental conditions by remote management of vehicle maintenance and service schedules and automatic on-board software updates (Over-The-Air – OTA), communication of V2X type (Vehicle-to-Everything) enabling interaction with road infrastructure and other road users. In this context, telematics is the foundation for the development of intelligent vehicles and autonomous systems that integrate AI, Big Data, IoT, and edge computing technologies.

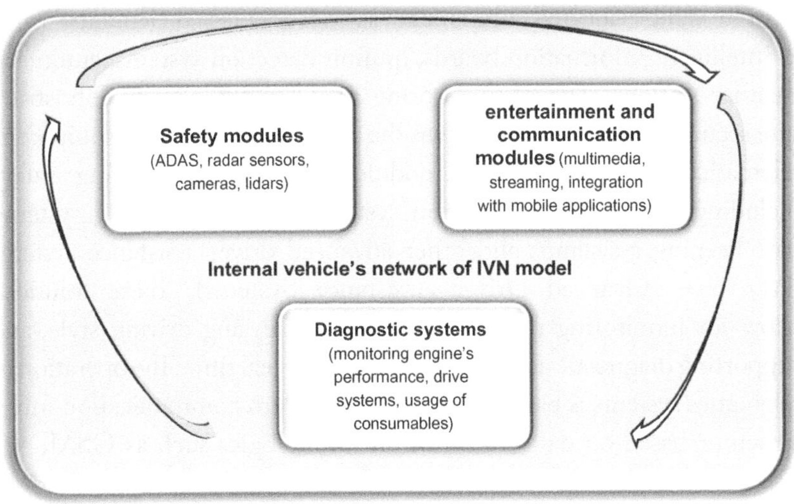

Figure 3.10 The IVN model's internal vehicle network which connects various system components.

Source: Own elaboration.

The development of telematics has also an economic dimension. On the one hand, it creates new revenue streams for vehicle manufacturers and service providers – for example, through subscription models (update subscriptions, access to advanced features, premium services). On the other hand, telematics systems contribute to achieve social and environmental goals – by reducing CO2 emissions, optimizing travel times, improving transport safety, and reducing the number of road accidents. IVN, as a concept of future architecture, redefines the role of the vehicle in the transport ecosystem, transforming it from an isolated transport unit into an intelligent, communicating element of an integrated mobility infrastructure.

3.3 Structure, Operation and Applications of Telematics Systems in Transport Companies

Telematics systems in road transport companies are complex and multidimensional technological solutions that enable the integration of vehicles with road infrastructure and fleet management systems, providing access to real-time data. Modern telematics solutions include both in-vehicle-located components as well as external elements – such as intelligent information boards, motion detection systems, automatic weather stations, devices monitoring road conditions, and infrastructure securing roadwork sites. From the perspective of vehicle equipment, telematics systems integrate modules that support driving safety, including traffic sign recognition systems, collision warning systems, lane keeping assistants, and other advanced driver assistance systems (ADAS – Advanced Driver Assistance Systems). These solutions allow for monitoring driving parameters, analysing driving style, and supporting diagnostic and service processes in real time. The operation of telematics systems is based on the use of modern communication infrastructure, based on data transmission technologies such as GSM, 4G, TETRA, Wi-Fi, Bluetooth, fiber optics, and satellite communications (GPS, Galileo). These technologies enable fast and reliable data transfer between system components – both within the vehicle and between the vehicle and external infrastructure and the company's central systems. The key function of telematics systems in road transport is information management – from its acquisition from sensors and measurement devices, through processing in computer systems (on-board computers, central servers), up to presentation to the user in the form of analyses, reports, and visualizations. These processes are supported by advanced analytical tools such as GIS (Geographic Information Systems), fleet management platforms (FMS), and software for analysing and monitoring transport processes (Neumann, 2017, p. 5).

Examples of the use of modern telematics solutions in road transport companies include, e.g. Scania Fleet Management or GPS-Solid Security, which offer functions for monitoring vehicles' location, analysing drivers' driving style, controlling fuel consumption, monitoring exhaust emissions, and generating fleet efficiency reports. From a classification perspective, telematics systems used in road transport can be divided into three main categories (Figure 3.11).

Telematics systems are therefore a key tool supporting the operational activities of transport companies, enabling processes' optimization, improving safety, and effective fleet management in a complex and dynamic transport environment. Modern telematics systems in road transport are characterized by an increasing level of complexity, integration, and adaptability, which results from the need to meet

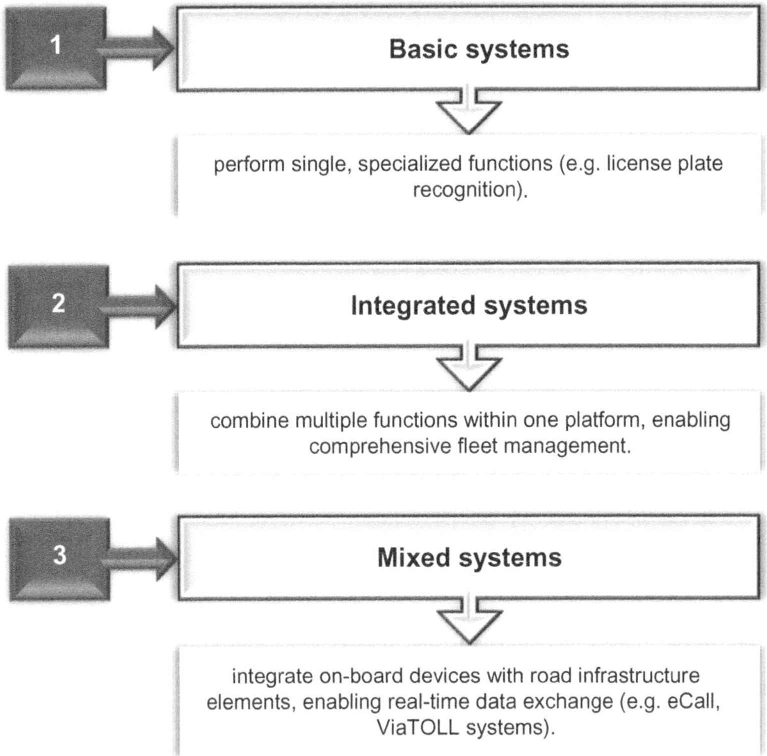

Figure 3.11 The three main categories for classifying telematics systems.

Source: Own elaboration.

dynamic market requirements, the complexity of logistics operations and the ongoing digitalization of the transport sector. A key determinant of their operational effectiveness is the ability to acquire, convert, interpret, and distribute data in real time, which enables making decisions based on current information about the condition of vehicles, road surroundings, weather conditions, logistics parameters, and so on.

Telematics, which initially served an auxiliary function supporting logistics processes, has evolved into a fundamental element of the digital transformation of the entire transport ecosystem, connecting vehicles, infrastructure, operational centres, and external systems into a coherent mobility management system. Functional analysis of modern telematics systems allows to distinguish three key technological areas (Figure 3.12).

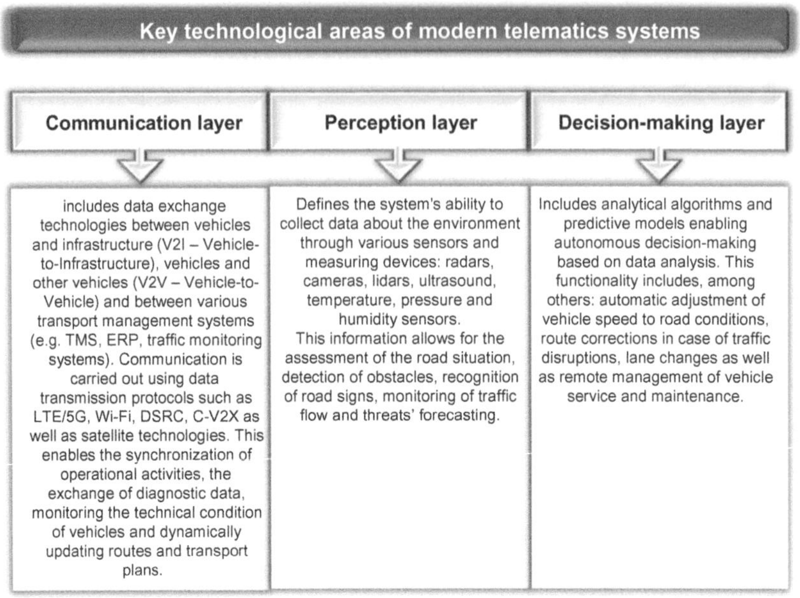

Figure 3.12 Three key technological areas of modern telematics systems.

Source: Personal studies.

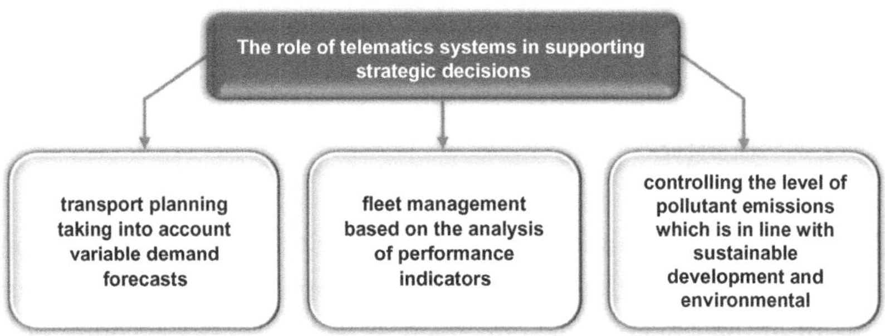

Figure 3.13 The role of telematics systems in supporting strategic decisions.

Source: Own elaboration.

Telematics systems, in addition to supporting operational functions (ongoing fleet monitoring, control of technical parameters, vehicles' location), play an increasingly important role in supporting strategic decisions – Figure 3.13.

Thanks to the ability to integrate data from multiple sources (on-board sensors, infrastructure devices, weather systems, logistics databases) and their contextual analysis, telematics systems are becoming the basis for modern models of intelligent mobility management. The architecture of these systems is evolving towards modularity, flexibility and interoperability, which allows for easy configuration and updating of services during vehicles' exploitation. Open API interfaces, communication standards (e.g. JSON, XML, MQTT), and programming platforms supported by ML and AI allow telematics systems to adapt to changing operating conditions – both at the level of a single vehicle and the entire fleet. Thanks to these properties, telematics is becoming a key element of the digital transport ecosystem, enabling the implementation of advanced predictive functions, dynamic response to changes in the operating environment, and supporting long-term strategies of sustainable development in road transport.

The dynamic development of telematics systems in road transport, which are an integral part of the more broadly defined intelligent transport systems (ITS), is an important element of the digitalization of operational processes in transport companies. The implemented solutions enable the integration of telecommunications technologies, information systems, transport management tools, and road infrastructure into one coherent ecosystem, supporting both operational and strategic activities. Of key importance for transport companies is the ability of telematics systems to integrate with advanced ITS infrastructure, which allows for effective planning and implementation of transportations in a dynamically changing road environment. These systems enable automatic adjustment of driving routes based on data from digital maps, traffic information, weather forecasts, and roadwork reports. By connecting with external data sources (such as traffic monitoring systems, weather stations, urban traffic management systems), telematics systems are transformed into platforms supporting real-time decision-making (Figure 3.14).

Telematics systems, through vehicle tracking, making drivers' driving style analysis, exhaust emission monitoring, and operational reporting, are a tool supporting the achievement of key operational goals of transport companies. They enable not only ongoing monitoring of transport operations, but also fleet efficiency analysis, maintenance planning, reduction of operating costs, and increase of transport safety.

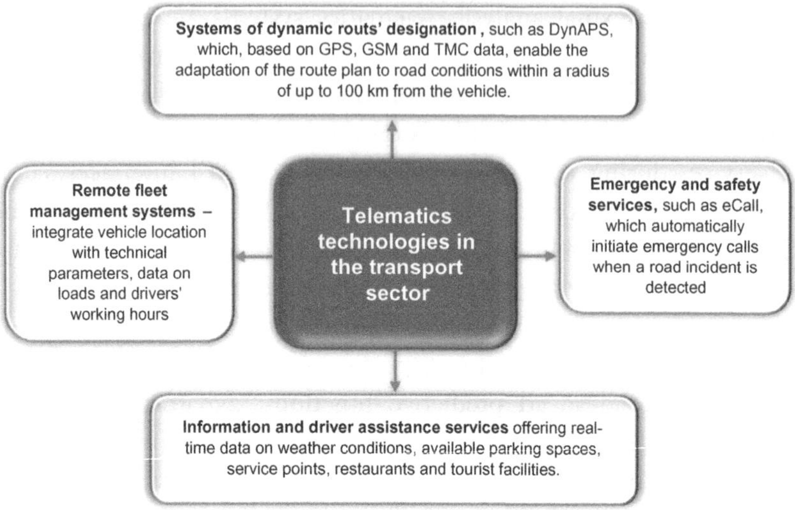

Figure 3.14 Examples of telematics technology implementations in the transport sector.

Source: Own elaboration.

The prospects for the development of telematics systems in transport companies include further integration with solutions of intelligent networked vehicles (Connected Vehicles) and automated driving systems. The capabilities of on-board terminals are also expected to expand from devices focused on monitoring functions towards multimedia-integrated information management centres that will combine diagnostic, operational and environmental data with entertainment and communication services.

The development of telematics systems in the transport sector not only supports the optimization of transport operations, but also contributes to the achievement of broader social and economic goals. These include, among others: reducing pollutant emissions, reducing the number of accidents, improving air quality in urban areas, shortening travel times, and increasing the competitiveness of transport companies through an innovative approach to fleet management and logistics processes. Thus, telematics systems are becoming not only an operational tool, but also a strategic component of the digital transformation of road transport companies, enabling adaptation to the challenges of the modern market, including the growing requirements in the field of sustainable transport, safety, cost efficiency, and integration with modern digital services in the frame of intelligent mobility.

From a systemic perspective, transport telematics is an integral element of the architecture of ITS, combining information, telecommunications, and engineering technologies into one coherent ecosystem supporting the implementation of complex transport processes. Its key function is to improve the transport of people and goods through the efficient use of existing transport infrastructure, minimizing the costs of expanding the physical road network, and limiting the negative impact of transport on the environment. The basic requirement of modern telematics systems is not only the use of advanced communication technologies, such as LTE, 5G, DSRC, C-V2X, or satellite communication (GPS, Galileo), but above all ensuring interoperability and architectural flexibility. This means the system's ability to support diverse services (e.g. navigation, fleet monitoring, operational data analysis) and users (transport companies, drivers, infrastructure operators, bodies of public administration) as well as to adapt to a dynamically changing transport environment – including variable weather conditions, diverse legal regulations, diverse vehicle technologies, and the infrastructure of multiple operators.

From a functional perspective, transport telematics systems operate within a complex, hierarchical architecture in which different levels of management and control perform specific tasks (Figure 3.15).

The implementation of these tasks requires reliable and efficient data transmission channels enabling communication between the physical components of the system (vehicles, roads, communication nodes,

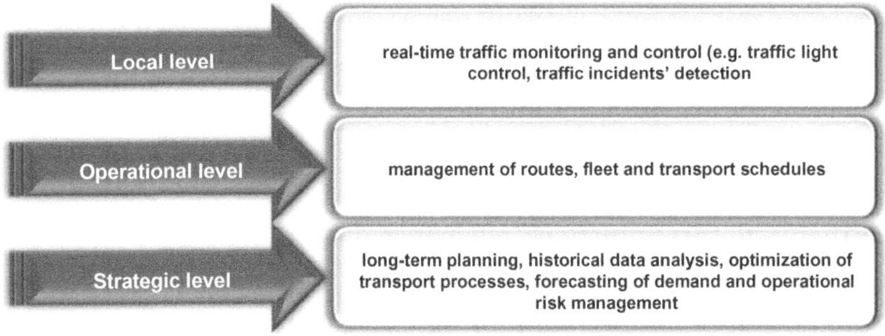

Figure 3.15 Levels of management and control of telematics systems in transport.

Source: Own elaboration.

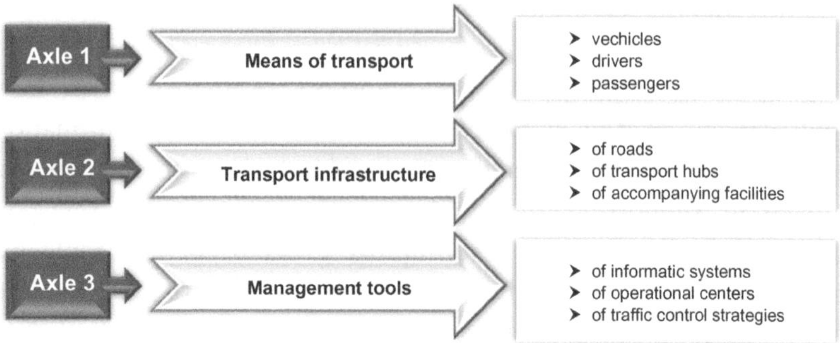

Figure 3.16 Division of telematics systems.

Source: Own elaboration.

sensors) and its digital layer (analytical software, control algorithms, users' interfaces).

The ITS organizational model, in accordance with the literature on the subject, assumes the division of the system into three main components' axes (Figure 3.16).

In this structure, telecommunications serves as a key transmission medium, enabling the smooth flow of information between various levels of the system – from detectors, sensors, and measuring devices, through data processing modules, to analytical centres, and decision-making centres. Telematics in transport companies, being part of a broader ITS ecosystem, allows for the implementation of solutions enabling ongoing fleet monitoring, analysis of technical parameters of vehicles, optimization of transport processes as well as increasing the safety and efficiency of transport through integration with road infrastructure and external traffic management systems. From a practical point of view, the applications of telematics systems in transport companies cover a wide spectrum of operational and strategic functions, supporting both traffic management and the optimization of logistics processes (Figure 3.17).

Thanks to these functions, telematics systems contribute to increase the operational efficiency of transport companies, increasing the level of transport safety, improving the quality of services provided, and increasing the comfort of transport users, including passengers using public transport. In a broader perspective, the development of

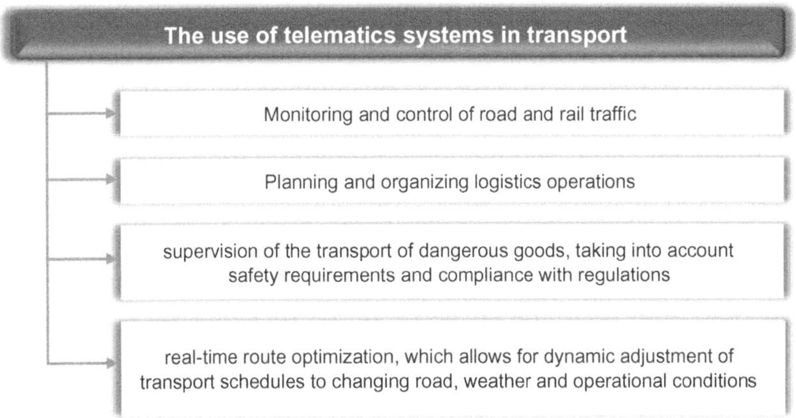

Figure 3.17 Examples of applications of telematics systems in transport.

Source: Personal studies.

telematics systems is seen as a key element in the implementation of European sustainable transport strategies, such as the construction and modernization of the Trans-European Transport Network (TEN-T). Investments in telematics systems play an important role in the integration of various modes of transport – road, rail, sea, and air – enabling their interoperability at the level of data, infrastructure, and operational processes.

Telematics management systems in transport companies are not only technological tools, but also important instruments of transport policy, supporting the achievement of goals in the field of sustainable mobility, reduction of greenhouse gas emissions, and the development of modern models of urban and regional logistics. Making usage of them allows for the implementation of an intelligent transport policy, in which the priority is not only to improve the flow of people and goods, but also to minimize the impact of transport on the natural environment and urban space. In this context, telematics is no longer perceived solely as a solution supporting traditional transport processes, but is becoming a fundamental pillar of modern traffic, infrastructure and supply chain management. It is a key element in building smart cities (Zelinka, 2013, p. 55). Modern telematics systems in road transport companies are no longer merely tools supporting selected operational aspects. They are increasingly being implemented as comprehensive platforms for managing transport processes, enabling the integration of many functions that are of key importance to the effective running of transport operations. To the basic functional areas of these systems should be included vehicle mileage records, fuel, and energy consumption monitoring, driver work time registration and analysis, operating cost control and real-time transport order processing. Modern transport telematics is therefore a multidimensional functional and information system whose main goal is not only to increase the efficiency of logistics processes, but also to improve transport safety, user comfort and sustainable management of infrastructure resources. The ongoing integration with advanced digital technologies is leading to the emergence of so-called intelligent transportation environments (ITE), in which the system architecture is based on the use of software agents – autonomous units capable of perceiving data, processing it and independently undertaking operational actions. Each agent within this architecture can independently respond to changes in the transportation environment, but its operations are integrated within a common system logic. This model enables dynamic adaptation to changing operational conditions, such as sudden changes in traffic volume, road accidents, weather conditions, or unplanned disruptions. At the heart of modern telematics architectures is the concept of distributed information management and decentralization of decision-making processes. This means that individual subsystems – dedicated to different areas of transportation management, such as traffic safety, emission control, fleet management, or fuel optimization-can function as autonomous modules, communicating within a unified system platform. To ensure the consistency and interoperability of the system, it is crucial to use unified communication protocols (e.g. MQTT, REST API, SOAP), which enables scaling the architecture, integration with external systems and implementation of new functionalities without the need to interfere with the physical infrastructure of the system. An important role in the design of such systems is played by the concept of service-oriented architecture (SOA), in which individual functions of the telematics system are implemented as independent, autonomous services (so-called: microservices). This approach allows for flexible system development – for example, adding functions for

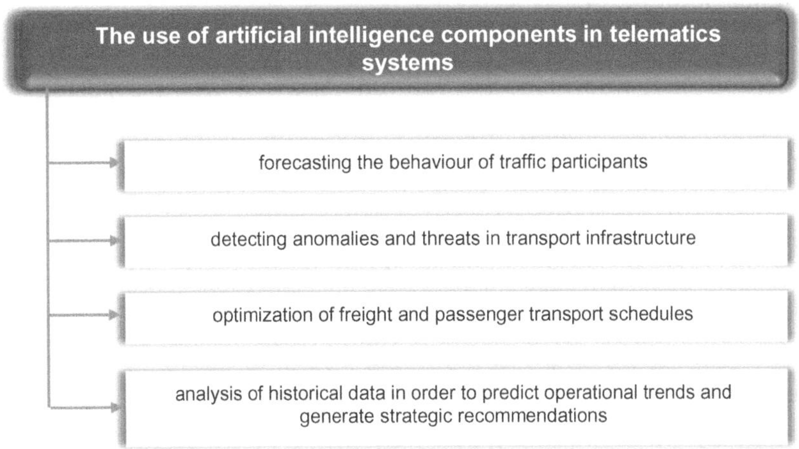

Figure 3.18 Abilities of telematics systems thanks to artificial intelligence components' usage.

Source: Own elaboration.

intelligent parking space management, dynamic fare pricing or route optimization taking into account weather data, and without the need to rebuild the entire IT infrastructure.

AI and ML components are also gaining increasing importance in telematics systems (Figure 3.18).

Telematics systems in transport companies become increasingly operate in the cloud computing model, which enables unlimited access to data, flexible scaling of computing power, as well as easy integration with external systems – both technological (e.g. ERP, TMS systems) and social systems (e.g. applications for passengers, city information systems). Data is transferred multi-directionally – between on-board devices and traffic management centres, but also directly between end users, who can exchange information about route conditions, disruptions, or random events, which increases the overall operational awareness of traffic participants and allows for the creation of crowdsourced traffic information systems. Technological transformation, including the development of telematics systems in road transport, has a direct impact on the practical operational aspects of transport companies. Modern telematics systems are no longer merely a technological backbone supporting individual operational processes – they are becoming a strategic management tool, integrating data about the vehicle, driver, route, cargo, and external conditions in a single environment. The ability of telematics systems to dynamically collect, analyse, and share information in real time opens up new perspectives in terms of optimizing logistics processes, minimizing operating costs, increasing the efficiency of using transport resources, and improving transport safety. Importantly, these systems are becoming an essential element of the information infrastructure of enterprises, enabling effective operational and strategic decision-making based on reliable data. In the practical operation of road transport companies, the role of telematics systems is particularly evident in the context of challenges related to the dynamic market environment, growing competition, variability of orders, and the need to reduce costs and increase energetic efficiency. It is in these areas that the implementation of modern management information systems (IT), based on telematics solutions, becomes a key element of operational strategies supporting the daily activities of transport companies.

Modern road transport enterprises (RTEs) operate in a highly competitive and dynamically changing environment, which generates numerous operational and organizational problems (Verdonck et al., 2013, pp. 700–719). Meeting the challenges of competitiveness (Radovic, 2018, pp. 700–719) and striving for process optimization – especially in the area of fuel and energy efficiency (Hernandez et al., 2016, pp. 1540–1556) – requires the implementation of modern and effective operational strategies (Crainic et al., 2009, pp. 541–557), that support taking up managerial decisions (Chatterjee, 1995, pp. 57–80),[5] especially in the area of managing daily operational activities (Schlote et al., 2015, pp. 275–284), (Joh et al., 2011, pp. 1245–1251). One of the solutions aimed at improving operational efficiency in the transport sector is the implementation of management information systems (IT), more broadly understood as telematics systems (Giannopoulos et al., 1997, pp. 37–59), (Xu, 2000, pp. 179–200). Their functionality includes, among others, recording vehicles' mileage, monitoring operating costs, fuel and energy consumption, analysing driver performance and handling transport orders (Janecki et al., 2010, pp. 43–49). Additionally, these systems enable the optimization of transport routes (Taniguchi et.al., 2003, pp. 301–322), (Spiekerman & Neubauer, 2002, pp. 9–11), (Ye et al., 2015, p. 555), and more efficient use of transport resources, such as vehicle capacity (Ning et al., 2013, pp. 105–110) or drivers' working time (Bäumler, Kotzab, 2017, p. 5), which is particularly important in conditions of irregular orders and changing customers' needs (Mondragon, 2009, pp. 229–240), (Quinet, Vickerman, 2008, pp. 350–353). The use of IT systems in the management of transport enterprises has become the subject of numerous discussions both among practitioners and management theoreticians. This debate is primarily about their importance, effectiveness, and role in the decision-making process aimed at improving operational efficiency in the economic, energetic and environmental context (Giannopoulos, 2009, pp. 147–161), (Kortum, 1998, pp. 133–144).[6] In the context of transport operations management, efficiency should be considered in conjunction with the development and implementation of telematics systems. Telematics – as a combination of information and telecommunications technologies – is used not only in monitoring and controlling transport processes but also as a tool supporting the assessment of the effectiveness, productivity and efficiency of RTEs. Modern telematics systems allow not only to collect data, but also to integrate it with management decision support tools, which makes them an important component in managing the efficiency of operational activities. Efficiency in transport services, considered from the perspective of the use of telematics systems, is a superior category to concepts such as capacity, profitability, productivity, effectiveness, flexibility, or rationality (Quinn & Rohrbaugh, 1983, pp. 273–393). In this approach, efficiency can be defined as the relationship between inputs and results (Cameron, 1986, pp. 513–644), the ability to quickly and accurately adapt to changes, as well as a measure of the organization's ability to achieve goals (McShane et al., 2000) and implement strategies (Aktas et al., 2011, pp. 1560–1573), which is also a tool for assessing the effectiveness of operations (Cameron, 2015). According to management theory, organizational effectiveness (Venkataiah, 2006, pp. 1–7), means the ability of a system – in this case the telematics system in RTE – to flexibly adapt to the environment and to effectively manage resources (e.g. fuel, energy) in order to achieve the assumed structure of goals (Cameron et al., 2983, pp. 477–478). Organizational efficiency consists of two main components: technical efficiency (Russell, 1985, pp. 109–126) and managerial efficiency (Ostroff & Schmitt, 1993, pp. 1345–1361), both of which are directly supported by properly designed and integrated telematics systems.

Technical efficiency refers to the effectiveness of technology being used and the scale of its application within an enterprise. According to the axioms of the transport market, the primary unit responsible for organizing transport processes is the RTE, which conducts operational activities in the field of transport services and evaluates its effectiveness through the lens of organizational efficiency (Nyulásziová & Palová, 2020, pp. 75–105) (Krasnyanskiy, Penshin, 2016, pp. 15–20). RTEs' operational activities are closely linked to the provision of transport services, in which the central element is the transport production processes (Grantner et al., 2010, pp. 336–342), encompassing the use of human resources, technical means, and energy materials (fuels, energy). Therefore, the primary criterion for the efficiency of transport processes is the efficiency of the realization of transport processes themselves (Kozhukhovskaya, Baskov & Ignatov, 2017, pp. 361–366). The latter one, can be measured using indicators such as: fleet technical availability, fleet utilization rate, operation of technically efficient vehicles, average daily vehicle operating time, operational time, capacity utilization, vehicle mileage, fuel consumption, and the others (Kovács, 2017, pp. 124–132). Telematics systems, thanks to the integration of data from vehicles and infrastructure, enable continuous tracking of these indicators and their ongoing reporting. In turn, management efficiency concerns the efficiency of decision-making by management staff, the effects of which directly influence the operational efficiency of RTEs (Cějka et al., 2016, pp. 98–101; Dubrovsky et al., 2016, pp. 389–412). Telematics systems, by providing data on vehicle utilization, driver driving style, working time and fuel consumption, support managers in making faster, more accurate and analytically justified decisions. Management effectiveness translates directly into the perception of the company by customers and its image (Nakano, 2017, pp. 3769–3788; Durišova et al., 2019, p. 6164). The measures of management effectiveness assessment include, among others, decision-making competences of the management, decision-making time, the scope of system support (including the use of telematics) and the correctness of decisions, assessed on the basis of evaluation systems and decision theory (Radović, 2018, p. 434; Bokovets et al., 2017, pp. 27–32;

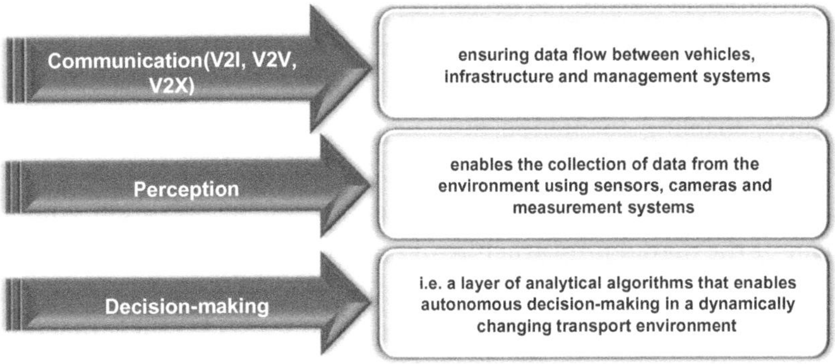

Figure 3.19 Key elements of telematics systems.

Source: **Own elaboration.**

Kalinichenko et al., 2019, pp. 241–254). Telematics systems in road transport companies are complex, multi-dimensional technological tools that integrate vehicles, road infrastructure, management centres and information systems into one coherent ecosystem supporting the management of transport processes. Their main goal is to improve operational efficiency, optimize the use of resources, increase transport safety and reduce negative impact on the environment. Modern telematics systems are no longer just tools supporting individual operational processes – they are becoming strategic components of the digital transformation of the transportation sector. Their role extends beyond fleet monitoring and determining vehicle location to include advanced analytical and predictive functions as well as real-time management decision support (Figure 3.19).

The ability of telematics systems to integrate with information and telecommunication technologies, including ERP and TMS systems, cloud platforms, and external data sources, enables comprehensive management of logistics processes, cost optimization, and support for long-term sustainable development strategies. Telematics systems in transport companies enable not only monitoring fuel consumption, controlling drivers' driving style, and analysing technical parameters of vehicles, but also optimizing transport schedules, managing fleets taking into account demand forecasts, controlling pollutant emissions, and minimizing operational risks. Their role in building intelligent transport environments and in creating smart city ecosystems as well as sustainable mobility is becoming crucial for the future of the road transport sector. Telematics systems are not only operational tools, but also strategic decision-support instruments in road transport companies, enabling adaptation to the challenges of the modern market, implementation of sustainable transport policies, and increased competitiveness in the TSL sector. Telematics systems are a key component of the digital infrastructure of modern road transport companies, integrating information, communication, and sensor technologies to monitor, analyse and optimise transport processes. I Their functionality goes beyond basic operational support – it enables real-time data collection, analysis of fleet operating parameters, costs' and emission control as well as supports strategic decision-making. The use of telematics contributes to increasing operational efficiency, minimizing risk, improving transport safety, and achieving sustainable development goals. Modern telematics systems are evolving towards solutions based on open architectures, modularity, and integration with external systems, which allows for flexible adaptation to changing market requirements and the management needs of transport companies.

3.4 Taxonomy of Telematics Systems and Modules in Road Transport Companies – Functional and Operational Approach

In the context of the large variety of telematics solutions available on the market, it is important to organize and classify the telematics systems and modules used. It will be made based on the example of car transport companies. Organizing these solutions into logical groups, according to specific criteria, allows for more efficient recognition, evaluation, and selection of appropriate systems depending on the operational needs. The taxonomy of telematics systems and modules not only facilitates the quick identification of the functions and capabilities of a specific solution but also enables its effective adaptation to the specific nature of transport activities. Telematics systems used in car transport include primarily non-telephone solutions enabling two-way data transmission between the operational headquarter and vehicles or other transport facilities in the field. Even in cases where the main effect for the end user is a one-way flow of information – e.g. data transfer from the vehicle to the control centre – the correct operation of the system requires establishing two-way communication for the transmission of data, confirmations, or parameter updates. The classification of telematics systems and modules can be based on many criteria, of which technical aspects are of significant importance – such as data acquisition methods, methods of their organization and transmission, information presentation technologies, the degree of processes' automation, and the types of devices collecting and processing data. This type of approach is particularly useful when analysing the possibilities of integrating telematics systems with the existing IT infrastructure in a transport company and when assessing technical aspects such as system compatibility, interface availability, or hardware requirements. In the context of the taxonomy of telematics systems and modules in road transport companies, it is worth emphasizing that the information value of divisions based on technical criteria depends primarily on their usefulness in the process of assessing the possibility of integrating a new system with the existing IT infrastructure of the company. In practice, although technological parameters – such as interfaces, communication protocols, or hardware compatibility – may be an important factor, at the same time they should not be the primary criterion for selecting a telematics system, especially in the case of large road transport companies.

Market experience shows that most modern telematics systems already offer standard or configurable solutions for communication with external IT systems (such as TMS, ERP, fleet management systems). The possibility of developing appropriate interfaces or adapting existing communication solutions is often available but requires careful analysis at the stage of implementation design. It is precisely defining the requirements for data exchange and ensuring reliable communication that is a key element of the success of implementing a telematics system in an enterprise.

In practice, more justified than relying on rigid, technical system classifications, is the approach based on the assessment of a specific system in terms of its compatibility with the existing IT infrastructure, the possibility of eliminating potential communication barriers, costs related to adaptation, and the time and resources necessary to realize the implementation. Therefore, in the process of selecting a telematics system, interdisciplinary cooperation is crucial – with the participation of technology, IT, logistics, and operational departments – in order to ensure that the selected solution will fully meet the specific needs of the company's operations. From the perspective of the operations of road transport companies – i.e. organizations implementing complex transport, logistics, and service processes – the classification of telematics systems and modules according to their functions and application in specific operational areas of the company is becoming crucial. This functionally and operational approach to taxonomy is also preferred by telematics systems' providers who adapt their offers to the real business needs of their customers, presenting modules and systems as sets of solutions dedicated to specific transport processes. The basic structure of the classification of telematics systems and modules, developed on the basis of the analysis of solutions available on the European market, is presented in the diagram in Figure 3.20.

One of the fundamental groups of telematics systems from a functional and operational perspective are localization systems and modules, which play a key role in monitoring the position of vehicles, loads, and – in some cases – drivers. These are solutions characterized by a low level of technical complexity, simplicity of installation and relatively low costs of purchase, implementation, and operation. These modules are widely available on the market as compact devices-standalone or powered by the vehicle's electrical system-that can be easily installed in various transport units, such as tractor-trailers, semi-trailers, or trailers. Their versatility and affordability make them particularly attractive to smaller transport companies that require basic telematics system functionality without advanced analytical options or without integration with other modules. This group of solutions also includes mobile phone-based location systems that enable the driver's or vehicle's position to be determined by activating a mobile application that sends location data to the headquarter. It is worth emphasizing, however, that the implementation of simple location systems, especially those based on the geo-positioning of people (e.g. drivers), requires taking into account legal provisions regarding personal data protection and information obligations towards employees. Furthermore, in the case of basic geolocation systems, data from vehicles is usually transmitted to the system provider's central databases, and the end user gains access to it via web applications operating in the SaaS (Software as a Service) model. This means that vehicle location data is shared via external

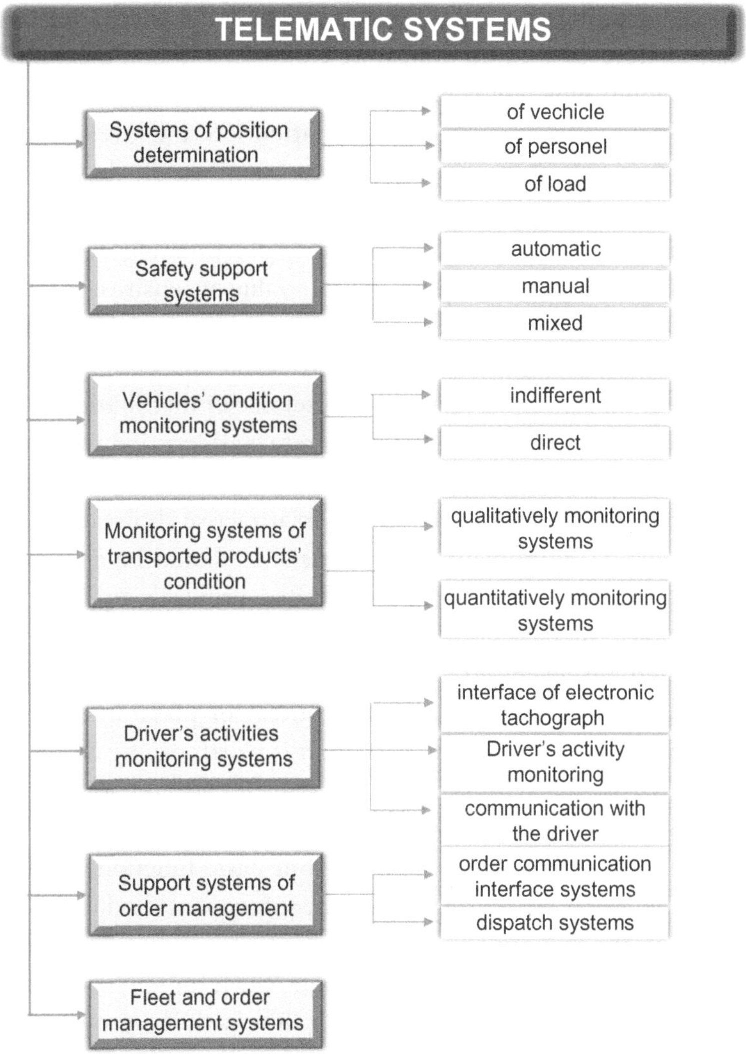

Figure 3.20 Taxonomic division of telematics systems for road transport companies.

Source: Own elaboration.

servers and visualized with the usage of publicly available online maps. Within the localization modules, the functional division according to the area of application is important, which includes three basic categories: vehicle geolocation systems, cargo geolocation systems, and personnel location systems.

The choice of a specific subsystem depends on the priorities and specific nature of a given transport company's operations – it is a decision about which elements of the transport unit (vehicle, driver, transported goods) require the most attention and oversight from management staff. These preferences vary significantly depending on the company's business profile. For example, courier operators may focus primarily on tracking shipments and estimating drivers' location, while companies transporting high-value or sensitive goods (e.g. pharmaceuticals, fuels, ADR goods) will pay more attention to vehicle and cargo monitoring in order to ensure safety and to minimize risk. In turn, companies offering additional service or distribution services may need complex solutions that integrate staff location with service processes. For many companies, especially those seeking basic telematics solutions, location modules are an attractive choice due to their simplicity and low implementation costs. It should be emphasized, however, that their functionality is limited primarily to basic operational tasks, such as location monitoring or generating mileage reports, without advanced analytical capabilities or integration with other management systems. In the context of planning long-term development of the telematics system, it is worth paying attention to the modular approach to system architecture design. The solutions that treat geolocation as one of the elements of a larger, scalable platform allow one to begin implementation from basic functions, and then successively expanding the system with subsequent modules, such as monitoring the technical parameters of vehicles, driving style control of drivers, or managing transport orders. Such an approach enables the system to be gradually developed in line with the growing needs of the enterprise, without the need to replace the entire technological infrastructure. Another key category in the classification of telematics systems for road transport companies are safety monitoring systems, which are responsible for early detection and response to potentially dangerous situations during transport. These solutions are designed to operate in a reactive operating mode – they operate passively until pre-defined events occur, after which they automatically initiate programmed safety procedures. From a technical point of view, safety monitoring systems allow for programming of activation conditions – such as exceeding a specific threshold value (e.g. of speed, pressure, standstill time) or the occurrence of defined events (e.g. entry into a prohibited zone, unauthorized unloading of goods, and so on). Until the trigger condition is met, the system remains in standby mode, without generating reports or notifications. At the time of activation, the system automatically carries out defined reactions, such as sending SMS notifications, e-mail messages, launching the alarm in the parent system, and in the case of more advanced solutions-also taking action directly on the vehicle, e.g. activating pump blockade, power cut-off in specific electrical circuits, or turning off devices not related to driving safety.

A special subgroup of security systems are modules managing the release of products, which enable the implementation of geographical blockades – e.g. blocking the possibility of unloading fuel outside specific geographical points, which provides protection against unauthorized access to goods being transported. The most frequently used parameters that may constitute the basis for activating safety systems in the practice of road transport companies include, among others:

- entry into (or exit from) a specific geographical area (e.g. leaving the designated route, vehicle's appearance in a prohibited zone, stopping in places with an increased risk of unauthorized unloading),
- exceeding a certain speed, which is particularly important in special transport or in the case of a speed limit policy as a part of a fleet safety strategy,
- activation of loading or unloading systems at locations other than approved distribution points,
- recording sudden maneuvers, such as sudden braking, which may signal an emergency situation or accident.

Safety monitoring systems, although they operate in a reactive mode, play an extremely important role in the context of protecting the company's resources – both property (vehicles, cargo) as well as the safety of staff – drivers. Their use enables rapid response to incidents, increases the level of operational security and supports prevention in the context of potential threats such as theft, unauthorized unloading, or improper use of vehicles. As part of road safety monitoring systems, manual and hybrid modules are also distinguished, which enable drivers to actively report a threat situation through the alarm button installed in the vehicle. Activating this button initiates a pre-defined safety procedure, allowing the operational centre to quickly take protective action – for both the vehicle and the driver. For systems of this type to operate effectively and to fulfil their function in the operational practice of road transport companies, it is necessary to develop detailed safety procedures and communication schemes corresponding to various threat scenarios. The implementation of such a system involves a number of design activities, including:

- Analysis of risks related to fleet exploitation, including identification of potential threats to the driver, vehicle, and cargo.
- Hardware selection and configuration, including the strategic placement of alarm modules and activation buttons within the vehicle, with consideration given to their discreet location (e.g. out of an attacker's line of sight). Providing an independent power source is also crucial – for example, standalone batteries or emergency systems that will ensure the operation of alarm modules even in the event of a power outage to the vehicle's main power supply.

Defining logic of the system, i.e. determining system's behaviour in various operational scenarios:

- Standard mode – e.g. sending periodic reports confirming the absence of danger, colour marking of vehicles on the dispatch system map.
- Threat mode – specifying whether the alarm should be visible to a potential attacker (e.g. sound or light signals) or act as a "silent alarm" (without visible signs to bystanders). Of a key importance in this case, is to program communication procedures: the form of the report (in the form of SMS, e-mail or e.g. system signal), data transmission channels, list of notifications' recipients, method of informing the driver about the receipt of the report, and about the actions taken, together with the status of the intervention.
- Establishing a process for responding to an alarm signal, including procedures for verifying the report, confirming

the threat, transferring information between operational departments and the driver, as well as procedures for closing the alarm report after the threat has ceased.

In the context of the taxonomy of telematics systems, safety monitoring systems are an important element supporting risk management in road transport, enabling a quick response to crisis situations and securing transport processes against the effects of random incidents. Their effectiveness, however, depends not only on technology, but above all on properly defined operational procedures and adapting the system configuration to the specific nature of the company's operations. Modern road transport companies are increasingly faced with challenges related to the growing security threat resulting from both the dynamic geopolitical situation in Europe and the risk of terrorist incidents. Past experiences, such as the use of heavy goods vehicles for attacks, highlight the need for undertaking preventive measures to protect personnel, the transport fleet, and the cargo being transported from potential threats. In this context, telematics safety monitoring systems become not only a tool supporting daily operational activities, but also an element of strategic importance, enabling the reduction of operational risk. The implementation of such solutions in the structure of transportation company may bring measurable benefits, including the possibility of negotiating more favourable conditions for fleet, transport, and valuable loads. It is worth emphasizing that in the process of planning the implementation of security monitoring systems, early involvement of the insurer is crucial – this allows for the joint definition of requirements regarding the level of security, as well as the development of cooperation procedures in the event of incidents. Thanks to this, safety monitoring systems not only support operational security, but also fit into the risk management strategy, constituting an important element of the safety policy of road transport companies. Their implementation is not only a response to current threats, but also an investment in the future organizational resilience of the company, allowing for increased customer trust, reduction of insurance costs, and building a competitive advantage on the market. Another important group within the classification of telematics systems in road transport companies are vehicles' technical condition monitoring systems. These modules provide the information

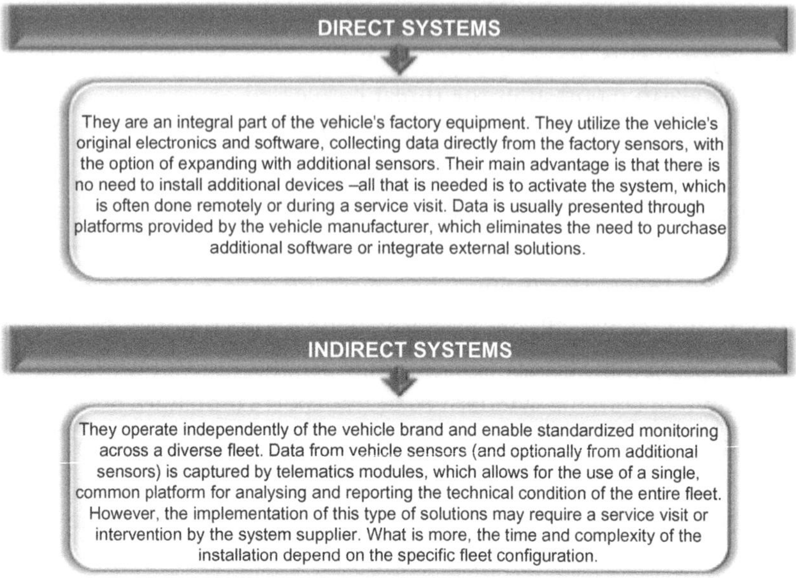

Figure 3.21 Vehicles' condition monitoring systems.

Source: Own elaboration.

necessary to maintain the technical efficiency of the fleet, minimize the risk of breakdowns and optimize operating costs. Vehicle condition monitoring systems can be divided into two basic categories – see Figure 3.21.

For fleet managers and service departments, it is crucial to be able to obtain a uniform, clear picture of the technical condition of all vehicles, regardless of the brand or age of the fleet. Therefore, direct systems are the natural choice for homogeneous fleets, while indirect systems, which ensure data consistency, are the natural choice for diverse fleets. Vehicle condition monitoring systems can serve as a simple diagnostic tool, limited to displaying basic data from sensors, or as an advanced management solution that enables comprehensive fleet management. Advanced systems enable monitoring of the entire vehicle lifecycle: monitoring technical condition, managing consumables, and spare parts, scheduling inspections, and archiving service history and technical documentation. Modern vehicle condition monitoring systems are evolving towards predictive maintenance solutions – predicting potential failures based on analysis of historical data and component wear patterns. This allows you to predict a failure, planning service activities in advance and minimize the risk of downtime resulting from sudden failures. Effective use of the vehicle's condition monitoring systems contributes to reducing operating costs, reduced risk of failure on the road as well as increasing the reliability and availability of the fleet for the operational needs of the company.

Another important category within the classification of telematics systems are systems for monitoring the condition of the transported product. Their main purpose is to ensure continuous monitoring of the quality and quantity of transported goods, which is of crucial importance in the operational activities of road transport companies, where transport settlements are based precisely on accurate cargo data. Traditional methods of securing goods, such as sealing valves and gates, recording parameters after completing transport or documenting loading and unloading processes, although useful, do not allow for ongoing monitoring of transport conditions and do not guarantee control over critical parameters such as temperature, humidity, or pressure. Telematic systems bring a completely new quality in this respect, enabling continuous monitoring of the condition of the carried load, which translates into a reduction in the risk of complaints, increasing the transparency of processes and better protection of the interests of the company and its clients. Within this group, two basic types of solutions can be distinguished:

a) Products' quality monitoring systems – based on a network of sensors installed in transport units, which allow for the ongoing measurement and transmission of data on key products' parameters, such as temperature, humidity, and pressure. This data can be automatically sent to headquarters or made available to customers to ensure full transparency of the transport process. The implementation of such systems requires precise adaptation to the needs of a specific company and its customers – determining the accuracy of measurements, the frequency of sending reports, alarm thresholds and procedures for responding to deviations from standards which have been established previously.
b) Product quantity monitoring systems – focus on supporting processes related to the documentation of loading and

unloading goods being transported. The selection of the appropriate system depends on the specific nature of the products being transported: different solutions work well for liquid cargo, different ones for bulk cargo, and still others for solid cargo. The key function of these systems is to ensure quantitative consistency between the transport order and the actual loading and unloading.

Quantity monitoring systems can therefore support both documentation processes and the protection of shipments against loss or theft. It should be emphasized that the implementation of the product monitoring systems requires a thorough analysis of the company's needs – determining which parameters must be monitored in real time, which data transfer intervals are sufficient, and which information can only be sent in the event of irregularities. Only this approach guarantees that the telematics system will actually support the company's operational processes and will not become merely a source of redundant, unnecessary data. The use of telematics solutions to monitor the condition of transported goods is particularly important in the context of transports, where possible complaints related to the quality or quantity of the delivered product may generate high logistic, operational, and financial costs. Continuous monitoring enables early detection of potential problems and the generation of documentary evidence that can be crucial in resolving disputes with customers or contractors. Additionally, quick access to cargo data supports settlement processes, accelerating document flow, and improving the company's financial liquidity. Ensuring the quality and integrity of transported goods is a key operational area, determining the security of logistics processes and the financial stability of the company. In car road transport, the risk of irregularities and potential complaints is much higher, which is due to the greater distances between the place of loading and the place of unloading, as well as the greater number of intermediate links in the supply chain. Any discrepancies in the condition or quantity of the delivered goods may lead not only to losses in the value of the cargo itself, but also to additional logistics costs, handling complaints, and even to delays in deliveries to subsequent recipients. For this reason, the implementation of telematics systems monitoring the condition of transported goods is becoming a key preventive tool, enabling not only ongoing monitoring of transport conditions, but also documenting the compliance of the transport process with customer requirements. Recording and archiving data from sensors monitoring the quality and quantity of transported cargo allows to create reliable documentation that can serve as evidence in potential disputes with contractors.

The particular importance of these solutions is visible in companies that bill their services based on the quantity of transported goods, which is measured during unloading. Telematic load monitoring systems enable precise and dynamic obtaining data on the amount of goods supplied which accelerates settlement processes, minimizes the risk of errors and supports operational continuity. Thanks to this, it is possible to shorten the billing cycle, which translates into improving company's financial liquidity and reduce the costs associated with the service of complaints or disputes arising from transport incompatibilities.

Another important group as part of the classification of telematics systems used in car road transport are driver activity monitoring systems. These solutions integrate data from electronic vehicle systems with additional functions of external modules, enabling comprehensive support for management processes of personnel driving fleet vehicles. These systems serve as key tools supporting the monitoring, analysis and optimization of driver performance, which is particularly important in the context of growing regulatory requirements and the desire to improve the operational efficiency of transport companies. Within this category, three basic subgroups of drivers' activity monitoring systems can be distinguished – see Figure 3.22.

Driver activity monitoring systems are therefore a key component of the telematics architecture of road transport companies, enabling not only the control of drivers' work compliance with regulations but also the analysis of driver performance, the identification of areas requiring optimization, and support for decision-making processes in the area of human resource management. For road transport companies operating in a complex and dynamically changing environment, precise knowledge of the current status of drivers is a key element of operational management. This information not only enables short-term planning of transport tasks, but also allows for the optimization of the use of available human resources in the context of the applicable regulations governing drivers' working time in Europe. The importance

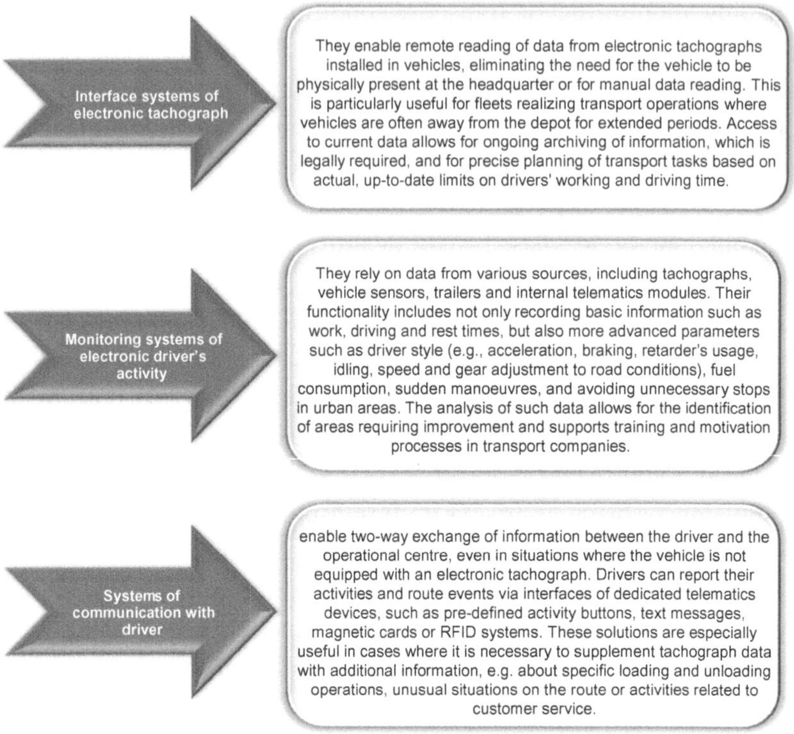

Figure 3.22 Basic subgroups of driver's activity monitoring systems.

Source: Own evaluation.

of this data increases especially in the area of work planning in road transport, where violation of legal standards can lead to financial and reputational sanctions as well as badly affect safety and operational performance. When selecting and implementing telematics systems to support human resource management, it is crucial to match the scope and detail of the data to the actual needs of the company. It is not enough to simply monitor the current status of drivers; it is necessary to obtain comprehensive information, such as remaining available working time, use of time limits on a weekly, fortnightly, monthly, and bimonthly basis, degree of use of extended driving time opportunities, dates of taking reduced rest periods. Access to such data in real time allows for more effective route and order planning, as well as avoiding the risk of violating regulations on drivers' working hours. Due to the complexity of the data processed, the process of selecting the right driver activity monitoring system requires close cooperation with dispatch and logistics departments, which have operational knowledge of the specifics of drivers' work, applicable regulations, and customer expectations. Only the inclusion of specialists from these areas allows the selection of solutions that are optimally tailored to the needs of the organization. Telematics systems with driver activity monitoring capabilities are therefore not only a tool for ensuring regulatory compliance, but also a strategic support element for optimizing operational processes in road transport. Making usage of them contributes to increasing fleet utilization, reduction of operating costs and improving the overall efficiency of transport operations.

Another important category of telematics systems used in road transport companies is solutions supporting the management of transport orders. Their main purpose is to increase the level of control over the execution of customer orders by ensuring efficient communication between the operations centre and the vehicles of the fleet. These systems enable bidirectional information flow – not only in terms of current order execution, but also in the transmission of new transport orders, status reporting, and preparing documentation of completed operations. In the context of road transport, order management systems are becoming a key tool, eliminating the limitations of traditional communication channels, such as telephone calls, sending documents by post or direct transfer of information at the operational base. Traditional methods generate a number of problems, such as the risk of errors in data transmission, delays in updating order statuses, and safety risks when making phone calls while driving. For transport companies that do not have dedicated dispatch systems, telematics modules supporting order management can be a beneficial alternative, facilitating ongoing operations, improving communication with drivers, and shortening the response time to changes in the transport plan. It is worth noting that the market also offers mixed systems that combine various functions in a single platform – from fleet and order management to technical monitoring of vehicles and driver activity. These comprehensive solutions are characterized by a high degree of scalability, the ability to configure them according to the company's needs, and advanced features for automating logistics processes. Thanks to this, they not only enable effective management of current operational activities, but also support the implementation of long-term strategic goals in the area of fleet management and customer service. Advanced telematics systems supporting order management in road transport companies offer an increasingly wide range of functionalities, including the ability to automatically assign orders to individual transport units. These types of solutions change the existing model of the dispatch department, which was traditionally responsible for manual route planning, transport sequence planning, and assigning orders to vehicles. In the new system, the role of dispatch staff shifts towards administrative tasks, primarily related to monitoring current data such as fleet status, customer information, and parameters of ongoing shipments. Decision-making functions such as order allocation and route optimization are, however, handled automatically by system algorithms. The high level of sophistication of these systems often involves the possibility of expanding interfaces and integrating with external modules. This allows the system to be tailored to the specific needs of the company, for example, by adding additional functions or integrating with other telematics systems. In practice, depending on the supplier and market strategy, companies may decide to purchase individual telematics modules, sets of modules or comprehensive platforms offering a defined range of functions within a single application.

In summary, the classification of telematics systems according to their use in the operational and management processes of road transport companies is a practical approach enabling the selection of solutions best suited to the needs of a given organization. However, the variety of technologies available on the market makes the process of selecting a telematics system complicated, time-consuming, and requires thorough analysis – both in terms of assessing the initial situation and the needs of the company, as well as the capabilities of available solutions and implementation aspects. The taxonomy of telematics systems includes, among others, vehicle geolocation modules, systems for monitoring technical condition of the fleet, transport safety, quality and quantity of transported cargo, drivers' activity and tools supporting the management of transport orders. The importance of flexibility, scalability, and interoperability of these systems, as well as their impact on operational efficiency, transport safety, and the possibility of integration with broader solutions within digital logistics ecosystems has been emphasized.

Notes

1 Nowacki G., *Telematyka transportu drogowego*, ITS. Warszawa, 2008.
2 Neumann, T. (2017). Wykorzystanie systemów telematyki na przykładzie wybranych przedsiębiorstw transportu drogowego. *Autobusy: technika, eksploatacja, systemy transportowe*, *18*(12).
3 Jetzke, S. *Grundlagen der modernen Logistik: Methoden und Lösungen*, Hanser Verlag, München 2007, p. 17.
4 Szulc, W. (2006). Elektroniczne metody monitorowania ruchomych środków transportowych (Electronic Methods of Monitoring Mobile Means of Transport). Warsaw Technical University, Transport Department. www.zabezpieczenia.com.pl/doz%C3%B3r-wizyjny/elektroniczne-metody-monitorowania-ruchomych-%C5%9Brodk%C3%B3w-transportowych-cz-1, data dostępu 1.05.2025.
5 Rosaldo, J.F.; Liu, R.R. An Agent-Based Approach to Assess Drivers' Interaction with Pre-Trip Information Systems. *Journal of Intelligent Transportation Systems*, 2005, 9, 1–10; 6. Sussman, J.S. Perspectives on Intelligent Transportation Systems (ITS); Springer: Boston, MA, USA, 2005; ISBN 978-0-387-23260-7.
6 Kapsalis, V.; Fidas, C.; Hadellis, L.; Karavasilis, C.; Galetakis, M.; Katsenos, C. A Networking Platform for Real-Time Monitoring and Rule-Based Control of Transport Fleets and Transferred Goods. In Proceedings of the 13th International IEEE Conference on Intelligent Transportation Systems – (ITSC 2010), Funchal, Portugal, 19–22 September 2010; pp. 295–300.

References

Aktas, E., Çiçek, I., Kıyak, M. (2011), The effect of organizational culture on organizational efficiency: The moderating role of organizational environment and CEO values, *Procedia-Social and Behavioral Science*, vol. 24, 1560–1573.

Bäumler, I., Kotzab, H. (2017), Intelligent transport systems for road freight transport – an overview, [in:] Freitag, M., Kotzab, H., Pannek, J. (Eds.), *Dynamics in logistics. Lecture notes in logistics*, Berlin, Heidelberg: Springer.

Bokovets, V.V., Zamkova, N.L., Makhnachova, N.M. (2017), Assessment of the effectiveness of enterprise management components in modern conditions, *Scientific Bulletin of Polissia*, no. 4, part 2, 27–32.

Cameron, K. S. (1986), Effectiveness as paradox: Consensus and conflict in conceptions of organizational effectiveness, *Management Science*, vol. 32, no. 5, 539–553.

Cameron, K. (2015), *Organizational effectiveness*, Wiley Encyclopedia of Management. Available online: https://doi.org/10.1002/9781118785317.weom110202 (last accessed: 28 July 2024).

Cějka, J., Telecký, M., Kolář, J. (2016), Appropriate strategies of transport companies for more efficient management with the aim of their further assessment using the operations research methods, *NAŠE MORE: znanstveni časopis za more i pomorstvo*, vol. 63, no. 3, 98–101.

Chatterjee, K. (1999), Modelling the impacts of transport telematics: Current limitations and future developments, *Transportation Reviews*, vol. 19, no. 1, 57–80.

Crainic, T.G., Gendreau, M., Potvin, J. Y. (2009), Intelligent freight-transportation systems: Assessment and the contribution of operations research, *Transportation Research Part C: Emerging Technologies*, vol. 17, no. 6, 541–557.

Dubrovsky, V., Yaroshevich, N., Kuzmin, E. (2016), Transactional approach in assessment of operational performance of companies in transport infrastructure, *Journal Industrial Engineering and Management*, vol. 9, no. 2, 389–412.

Durišová, M., Tokarcíková, E., Virlanuta, F.O., Chodasová, Z. (2019), The corporate performance measurement and its importance for the pricing in a transport enterprise, *Sustainability*, vol. 11, no. 21, 6164.

Giannopoulos, G.A. (2009), Towards a European ITS for freight transport and logistics: Results of current EU funded research and prospects for the future, *European Transport Research Review*, vol. 1, no. 4, 147–161.

Giannopoulos, G.A., McDonald, M. (1997), Developments in transport telematics applications in Japan: Traffic management, freight and public transport, *Transport Review*, vol. 17, no. 1, 37–59.

Grantner, J., Bazuin, B., Al-Shawawreh, J., Castanier, M. P., Hussain, S. (2010), Condition based maintenance for light trucks, [in:] Berthold, M. (Eds.), *Proceedings of the 2010 IEEE International Conference on Systems, Man and Cybernetics* 10–13 October 2010, Istanbul: IEEE.

Hernandez, A., Bernardo, M., Cruz, C. (2016), Relating open innovation, innovation and management systems integration, *Industrial Management & Data Systems*, vol. 116, no. 8, 1540–1556.

Janecki, R., Krawiec, S., Sierpiński, G. (2010), Telematics and the transportation system's value, *IFAC Proceedings Volumes*, vol. 43, no. 23, 43–49.

Joh, C.H., Lee, B., Bin, M., Arentze, T., Timmermans, H. (2011), Exploring the use of travel information–identifying contextual market segmentation in Seoul, Korea, *Journal of Transport Geography*, vol. 19, no. 6, 1245–1251.

Kalinichenko, A., Havrysh, V. (2019), Environmentally friendly fuel usage: economic margin of feasibility, *Ecological Chemistry and Engineering Studies*, vol. 26, no. 2, 241–254.

Kortüm, W., Goodall, R.M., Hedrick, J.K. (1998), Mechatronics in ground transportation-current trends and future possibilities, *Annual Review of Control*, vol. 22, 133–144.

Kovács, G.Y. (2017), Development of performance evaluation software for road freight transport activity, *Polish Journal of Management Studies*, vol. 15, no. 1, 121–134.

Kozhukhovskaya, L., Baskov, V., Ignatov, A. (2017), Modular management of indicators of efficiency and safety of transportation processes, *Transportation Research Procedia*, vol. 20, 361–366.

Krasnyanskiy, M., Penshin, N. (2016), Quality criteria when assessing competitiveness in road transport services, *Transportation Problems*, vol. 11, no. 4, 15–20.

McShane, S.L., Von Glinow, M.A. (2000), *Organizational behavior*, Boston: Irwin/McGraw-Hill.

Mikulski, J. (2010), Telematyka – przyszłość transportu i logistyki, *Logistyka*, vol. 2, 36–37.

Mondragon, A.E.C., Lalwani, C.S., Mondragon, E.S.C., Mondragon, C.E.C. (2009), Facilitating multimodal logistics and enabling information systems connectivity through wireless vehicular networks, *European Transport Research Review*, vol. 122, no. 1, 229–240.

Nakano, H.A. (2017), Study on the features of the evolution processes and business models of global enterprises in the transport sector, *Transportation Research Procedia*, vol. 25, 3769–3788.

Neumann, T. (2017), *Wykorzystanie systemów telematyki na przykładzie wybranych przedsiębiorstw transportu drogowego,* Autobusy: technika, eksploatacja, systemy transportowe, vol. 18, no. 12.

Ning, Y., Zhong-Qin, W., Ru-Chuan, W., Abdullah, A.H (2013), Design of accurate vehicle location system using RFID, *Elektron. Elektrotechnika*, vol. 19, no. 8, 105–110.

Nyulásziová, M., Palová, D. (2020), Implementing a decision support system in the transport process management of a small Slovak transport company, *Journal of Entrepreneurship, Management and Innovation*, vol. 16, no. 1, 75–106.

Österle, H., Winter, R. (2003), *Business engineering: auf dem weg zum unternehmen des informationszeitalters*, Heidelberg: Springer.

Ostroff, C., Schmitt, N. (1993), Configurations of organizational effectiveness and efficiency, *Academy of Management Journal*, vol. 36, no. 6, 1345–1361.

Quinet, E., Vickerman, R. (2008), *Principles of transport economics*, Cheltenham, UK: Edward Elgar Publishing.

Quinn, R.E., Rohrbaugh, J.A. (1983), Spatial model of effectiveness criteria: Towards a competing values approach to organizational analysis, *Management Science,* vol. 29, no. 3, 363–377.

Radović, D., Stević, Ž., Pamučar, D., Zavadskas, E.K., Badi, I., Antuchevičiene, J., Turskis, Z. (2018), Measuring performance in transportation companies in developing countries: A novel rough ARAS model, *Symmetry*, vol. 10, no. 10, 434.

Russell, R. (1985), Measures of technical efficiency, *Journal of Economic Theory*, vol. 35, no. 1, 109–126.

Schlote, A., Faizrahnemoon, M., Radusch, I., Crisostomi, E., Häusler, F., Shorten, R. (2015), A framework for real-time emissions trading in large-scale vehicle fleets, *IET Intelligent Transport Systems*, vol. 9, no. 3, 275–284.

Spiekerman, K., Neubauer, J. (2002), *European accessibility and peripherality: concepts, models and indicators*, Nordregio Working Paper: Stockholm, Sweden, 2002: www.diva-portal.org/smash/get/diva2:700463/FULLTEXT01.pdf (accessed on 28 July 2024).

Taniguchi, E., Yamada, T. (2003), Reliable vehicle routing and scheduling with time windows towards city logistics, [in:] Bell, M.G.H., Iida, Y. (Eds.), *The network reliability of transport*, Pergamon, Turkey: Emerald Group Publishing.

Venkataiah, P. (2006), Models of organizational effectiveness, *Osman Journal of Management*, no. 2. Available online: http://ou-mba.ac.in/i/3.pdf (accessed on 28 July 2025).

Verdonck, L. Caris, A., Ramaekers, K., Janssens, G. (2013), Collaborative logistics from the perspective of road transportation companies, *Transportation Reviews*, vo. 33, no. 6, 700–719.

Wydro, K.B. (2005), Telematyka-znaczenia i definicje terminu, *Telekomunikacja i techniki informacyjne*, vol. 1–2, 116–130 .

Xu, Y. (2000), Development of transport telematics in Europe, *GeoInformatica*, vol. 4, no. 2, 179–200.

Ye, N., Wang, Z., Zhang, Y., Wang, R., (2015), A method of vehicle route prediction based on social network analysis, *Journal of Sensors*, vo. 2015, no. 1, 210298.

Zelinka, T., Svitek, M., Votruba, Z., Jirovsky, V., Novak, M. (2013), *Transport Telematics-Systemic View*, Athens: WSEAS.

4

Ensuring the Safety and Security of Telematics Systems as a Strategic Challenge for Transport Management

4.1 Managing Risk of Telematic Systems in Logistics Companies

In describing the challenge of risk management, there are five types of risks identified (Engemann, 2019, pp. 26–35):

a) infrastructure risk,
b) enterprise risk,
c) information safety risk,
d) supply chain risk,
e) new technology risk.

In the transportation sector, modern, safe, protected, sustained, and rigid infrastructure plays a crucial role. It provides the foundation for efficient movement of people and goods, reduces the risk of accidents, and ensures continuity of services even under challenging conditions. Well-designed infrastructure also supports environmental goals by enabling greener modes of transport, lowering emissions, and encouraging the use of renewable energy. Moreover, investing in advanced transport infrastructure strengthens economic competitiveness, fosters regional integration, and improves the overall quality of life for society. Infrastructure resilience and risk management literature indicates that key decisions occur in the aftermath of adverse events. In this sense, proactivity, not reactivity is required. Logistics companies need to

DOI: 10.1201/9781003646518-5

prepare and communicate plans for securing the infrastructure beforehand in the event of a crisis or hazard (Marlow, Beale, Cook, Sharma, 2015, pp. 217–236).

Managing enterprise risk in logistics and taking quick decisions in order to secure stability, safety, and continuity is important. What is crucial is to look at a logistics company in a systematic and holistic approach. Unlike traditional risk management, where individual risk categories are managed separately – in a silo style, enterprise risk management (ERM) enables companies to manage risk in an integrated, enterprise-wide manner (Hoyt, Liebenberg, 2011, pp. 795–822). ERM, through a systematic and consistent approach (or process) to managing all risks faced by an organization, reduces the overall risk of company failure and thus increases the organization's efficiency and value. A carefully designed ERM programme can be a source of long-term competitive advantage and value through its macro-scale effects at the level of the entire company or business unit (Chudziński, Cyfert, Dyduch, Zastempowski, 2022). This raises some implications for logistics companies: a) risk management should concern the whole logistics system, b) strategic and managerial risk concerning decisions made during crises is as important as infrastructure risk, c) proper risk management can define future advantages.

Telematic systems are founded on safety and stability, and logistics companies are seen as strategically important. As a result, they are becoming increasingly aware of the necessity for information security, which is an increasingly important aspect of their business strategy. Using information security risk management (ISRM) to identify threats allows for the development of a security risk profile for critical assets in order to establish plans for dealing with threats in unexpected situations (Chudziński, Cyfert, Dyduch, Zastempowski, 2022).

Market globalization, shortened product life cycles, a reduced supply base, the need to slim down organizations, and the excessive use of outsourcing and offshoring contribute to increased supply chain risk management (SCRM), defined as a coordinated process among elements of the supply chain that reduces the likelihood of risky events and reduces the negative consequences for business after the occurrence of risky events. The most frequently mentioned supply chain risks also include those related to material, cash, and information flows. Uncertainty about the level of demand, unforeseen crises, and the weakness of individual links in the chain may cause fluctuations in product, material or services flows. In order to minimize such risks, a holistic approach to supply chain design coupled with proactive, systemic supply chain management is suggested. It is also important to identify the risks among suppliers and to determine which of them may fail during crises.

Technology risk is defined as the probability of physical, social, or financial losses due to the use of technologies and aggregated over the entire product life cycle. High impact technologies include large facilities, and they also include specific but widespread technologies, artificial intelligence and smart chips, as well as new communication devices. In order to reduce the risks related to the acquisition of new technologies, the following strategies are offered:

1) competitive benchmarking,
2) employee involvement, and
3) quality management.

It turns out that when implementing new technologies, organizations most frequently do not introduce practices related to risk reduction, such as risk identification, probabilistic risk analysis, planning with regard to uncertainty, analysis of cost-benefit trade-offs, or analysis of different risks related to different technologies. In contrast, business-to-business technologies linking the business activities of business partners, and increasing the dependence and interconnection between business partners' information systems, can increase the existing inter-company risk and create new risks (Chudziński, Cyfert, Dyduch, Zastempowski, 2022).

4.2 Standards and Recommendations for Managing System Security

Every telematics system combines telecommunications and informatics to monitor and manage vehicles or other assets. It uses GPS, different sensors, and wireless networks to collect, transmit, and analyse data, providing insights into vehicle location, driver behaviour, engine diagnostics, and more. This data is then used to improve fleet management, enhance safety, and optimize operations (Król, Rokicki, 2021, pp. 49–57).

Telematics systems gather data from various sources, sensors, and vehicle computers. The collected data are then transmitted wirelessly to a central platform for analysis. The platform analyses the data to provide many insights, such as vehicle location, driver behaviour patterns (speeding, harsh braking, etc.), engine performance, or maintenance needs. Due to the data collection and analysis, telematics systems are used in fleet management, vehicle tracking, insurance, and sometimes healthcare. The benefits of telematics systems are well described and embrace improved fleet management, enhanced safety, cost savings (e.g. on fuel), operations efficiency, and vehicle inspection reports.

As telematics systems connect together vehicles, road infrastructure, cloud platforms, and back-office logistics tools, they are prone to various cybersecurity risks. A single weak link – an unpatched vehicle gateway, an exposed API (Application Programming Interface, i.e. making an API accessible to other applications or systems for interaction), or an insecure over-the-air (OTA) update – can break down an entire transport network.

Thus, telematics systems security should rely on a multi-layered approach, encompassing secure data transfer, strong authentication, robust communication protocols, and regular security assessments. Key recommendations include implementing secure boot processes, digitally signing software updates, and using hardware-based security features. It is crucial to assume that code might be compromised and to design systems accordingly. Regularly testing and monitoring systems for anomalies is also essential.

Key standards and recommendations include secure data transfer, secure updates, hardware security, strong authentication, regular testing, etc. (Table 4.1).

To avoid common mistakes and to produce a secure system, there are some detailed guides on a secure development process that can prevent common design flaws. International standards, guidebooks, and norms serve two complementary goals: (i) they give transport managers a common language for risk governance, and (ii) they provide engineers with actionable, testable requirements from design

Table 4.1 Key Standards and Recommendations for Telematics System Security

Secure data transfer	Employ encryption and strong authentication protocols (like digital signatures or message authentication codes) to protect data during transmission between vehicles and external systems.
Secure boot mechanisms and updates	Implement secure boot mechanisms to verify the integrity of software and firmware before execution. Ensure software updates are obtained from authorized sources and are digitally signed to prevent tampering.
Hardware security	Utilize hardware-based security features like secure coprocessors to protect sensitive data and computations within the telematics system.
Operation plan in case of compromise	Design systems with the assumption that software or firmware might be compromised. Avoid relying solely on secrets embedded within the code for security. Have a plan when compromise happens.
Strong authentication	Implement strong authentication mechanisms for accessing telematics systems and data, using unique keys for different roles and functionalities. Authentication processes should be multi-layered, combining elements such as passwords, hardware tokens, and biometric verification to minimize the risk of unauthorized access. Furthermore, periodic key rotation and monitoring of access patterns are recommended to detect anomalies early and maintain the integrity of the system over time.
Regular testing	Conduct regular third-party audits and penetration testing to identify potential vulnerabilities. Monitor systems for unusual activity that could indicate a breach.
Secure design practices	Employ secure design principles throughout the development life cycle (minimizing attack surfaces, implementing secure coding practices, and adhering to industry best practices).
Communication security	Use secure communication protocols for all data transmitted between the vehicle and external systems. All exchanges of information should be encrypted end-to-end to prevent interception or tampering during transmission. Additionally, it is advisable to implement mutual authentication between communicating parties and to regularly update cryptographic algorithms in line with evolving security standards, ensuring the confidentiality, and integrity of data flows within telematics networks.
Monitor and react	Implement robust monitoring systems to detect and respond to security incidents (analysing system events and establishing incident response procedures).
Protect sensitive information	When collecting and using data, ensure compliance with privacy regulations and protect sensitive information. Data protection policies should clearly define the scope, purpose, and duration of data processing, minimizing the collection of personally identifiable information wherever possible. Moreover, anonymization and pseudonymization techniques, combined with strict access control, and regular security audits, should be applied to prevent misuse or unauthorized disclosure of sensitive data within telematics environments.

Table 4.1 (Continued)

Fleet management implications	Fleet managers should be aware of the data being collected and its potential implications for employee privacy and safety. Transparent communication with drivers and staff about the purpose and scope of data monitoring fosters trust and compliance with organizational policies. In addition, managers should establish clear internal procedures for data access, retention, and sharing, ensuring that collected information is used exclusively to enhance operational efficiency, safety, and regulatory compliance – without infringing on individual rights or privacy.

Source: Own elaboration.

through deactivating. The most significant guidelines for telematics are presented in Tables 4.2–4.5.

Combining a high-level governance framework (NIST CSF 2.0 or ISO 27001) with sector-specific standards (ISO/SAE 21434, UNECE R155, IEC 62443) creates a coherent, audit-ready security architecture for telematic systems. The strategic challenge is not the absence of guidance – but integrating overlapping requirements into clear policies, concise supplier contracts, and an operational-level playbook that frontline staff can actually follow. Below are some practical recommendations to develop a secure system:

1. Establish a tiered, multi-layered governance model. Use best practices and guidelines by the National Institute of Standards and Technology (NIST CSF "Govern"); implement an ISO 27001-certified Information Security Management System (ISMS) covering people–process–technology across the transport enterprise.
2. Adopt sector standards end-to-end: Use ISO/SAE 21434 TARA outputs to prioritize vehicle ECU hardening; propagate results into IEC 62443 security-zone definitions for depots and maintenance facilities.
3. Secure development and procurement: Require suppliers to show a Software Bill of Materials (SBOM) and evidence of secure-coding practices (e.g. MISRA, ISO/IEC 5055).
4. Secure continuous assurance: Map post-production monitoring requirements to your Security Operations Centre (SOC) run-books and to NIS2 (Network and Information

Table 4.2 Overarching Information-Security Governance: Frameworks, Regulations, and Guidelines for Telematics Systems Security Governance

LAYER	KEY STANDARD(S)	SIGNIFICANCE TO TELEMATICS
Enterprise Information Security Management Systems (ISMS)	ISO/IEC 27001:2022 – refreshed control set aligned with ISO 27002:2022; stronger focus on threat intelligence, cloud services and supplier relationships.	Most fleet-management platforms and traffic-control centres are SaaS/PaaS-hosted; a certified ISMS anchors contractual and regulatory assurance.
Risk management	ISO 31000; IEC 31010	Provides a vocabulary and toolbox that can be re-used in Threat Analysis and Risk Assessment (TARA) for vehicles.

Table 4.3 Road-Vehicle and Automotive Telematics

LIFECYCLE PHASE	MANDATORY / INDUSTRY-SPECIFIC GUIDANCE	NOTES FOR TRANSPORT OPERATORS
Governance & type approval	UNECE R155 – Cybersecurity Management System (CSMS) as a prerequisite for new vehicle types in 54 contracting parties since July 2022.	Even if you outsource vehicle acquisition, you must be able to demonstrate that your fleet meets R155 when operating across Europe/Asia-Pacific.
Engineering & development	ISO/SAE 21434:2021 – full life cycle cybersecurity engineering (concept → post-production) with mandatory TARA process.	Telematics control units (TCUs), V2X stacks, and OTA clients fall under ISO 21434 scope.
Best-practice guidebook	SAE J3061 – flexible process framework mapping security to ISO 26262 safety life cycle.	Still invaluable for mixed fleets (buses, trucks, off-highway) where ISO 21434 adoption is uneven.

Table 4.4 Cross-Sector Frameworks and Regulations

FRAMEWORK / REGULATION	TRANSPORT-SPECIFIC IMPACT
NIST Cybersecurity Framework v2.0 – now six core functions (Govern, Identify, Protect, Detect, Respond, Recover).	Offers a governance roadmap that can map ISO 27001 controls, 62443 technical measures, and 21434 work products into a single dashboard.
EU NIS2 Directive (2023/2555).	Extends mandatory risk management, 24 hour incident reporting, and supply-chain obligations to all medium/large transport & logistics operators in the EU by October 2024.

Table 4.5 Internet of Things (IoT) and Vehicle to Everything (V2X) Device Baselines

FRAMEWORK/ REGULATION	TRANSPORT-SPECIFIC IMPACT
ETSI EN 303 645 / TS 103 645	Offers an outcome-oriented baseline for connected devices (no default passwords, secure update, vulnerability disclosure).
Complements IEEE 1609.2	secure message format for DSRC/C-ITS) and 3GPP/5GAA specs for C-V2X credential management.

Source: Own elaboration.

Security Directive 2 (Directive (EU) 2022/2555), the updated EU directive establishing a high common level of cybersecurity across the European Union), incident-reporting KPIs.

5. Develop proper organizational culture and required competences: Train drivers, dispatchers, and maintenance crews on phishing, device-pairing hygiene, and "red-flag" indicators of telematics compromise; make this part of safety training.

In summary, building a truly secure telematics ecosystem requires more than compliance with individual standards – it demands their thoughtful integration into daily practice. A layered governance model, end-to-end adoption of sector frameworks, secure supply chain management, continuous monitoring, and a culture of security awareness together form a resilient defence against cyber threats. When translated into clear policies, enforceable contracts, and practical training, these measures ensure that security is not just a strategic aspiration but an operational reality across the transport enterprise.

4.3 Current State of Cybersecurity

Taking into account the need to increase the level of digital security and to increase the resilience of enterprises, including transport ones, to cyberattacks, it is becoming important to identify the types of cyberattacks and their sources. Cyberattacks, which involve an attack launched from one or more computers against another computer, multiple computers, or a network, take the form of identity theft, phishing, cyberbullying, manipulation to obtain valuable resources (including information and funds) as well as spam campaigns and the spreading of malicious files and software and infecting other systems. It is important to note that the use of malicious software (malware) can cause a computer or network to become inoperable, or the attacker may gain administrator access to the system to remotely control it. Ransomware is a type of malware that encrypts user files. In this case, the attacker demands a ransom to regain access to the data after payment. A specific form of cyberattack involves situation, in which an attacker is generating heavy traffic to a website, which significantly reduces the operational capacity of a company's systems and renders them inaccessible to users. Cyberattacks can target individuals, businesses, entire societies, and governments (Targowski, 2023, pp. 785–802).

In an era of increasing cyberattacks, which often take the form of cyberwarfare, digital security assessments play a crucial role. Penetration tests and simulated phishing attacks, as well as security audits and cyberattack vulnerability assessments, are used to assess this security. In this situation, employee training also plays a crucial role, aiming to raise awareness and shape employee attitudes and behaviours that are compliant with cybersecurity standards. This is especially important because many of the negative effects of cyberattacks are caused by employees' inappropriate responses to cyberattacks.

In this context, it's important to emphasize that cybersecurity has become a strategic priority for many businesses, including transportation companies, and not just a technical issue – the domain of IT departments. The scale, complexity, and serious consequences of cyberattacks necessitate a shift in perspective – from technical to business, from reactive to systemic. From the perspective of enterprises' managers, it is crucial to assume that an attack is already occurring or will occur soon, and that its consequences could impact the entire enterprise and its customers. Such an approach is gaining importance as enterprises increasingly encounter advanced persistent threat (APT) attacks. These attacks take the form of carefully planned, long-term operations that can go unnoticed for extended periods. They are particularly dangerous because they target less obvious infrastructure elements, such as integration points with vendor systems, cloud environments, and even applications used daily by employees. Cybersecurity and cyber resilience should therefore be perceived not as one-off projects, but as permanent competencies of the organization (Kurek, 2025, p. 55).

To-date, transport systems are more connected – and therefore more exposed to vulnerabilities in cybersecurity than ever before. As telematic platforms integrate cloud services, mobile connectivity, AI-based route optimization, and vehicle-to-everything (V2X) communications, they simultaneously inherit a growing number of cybersecurity vulnerabilities.

One can identify general environmental threats. First, logistics firms and transport operators are increasingly targeted due to their low downtime tolerance. Insecure VPNs, phishing, or lateral movement from IT systems can compromise telematics servers. Secondly, remote attack possibilities are expanding. Telematic Control Units (TCUs), cloud-based fleet-management portals, and OTA updates are accessible over public networks – creating more entry points. Thirdly, APTs have targeted critical infrastructure, including ports, rail, and air traffic control. Vehicle supply chains are now considered potential targets for disruption or espionage. Finally, cybercrime acts as a service (CaaS). Turnkey malware, stolen credentials, and exploit kits are now factors lowering the barrier for less sophisticated attackers.

There are also vulnerabilities specific for telematics, concerning the problem of connected trucks, using insecure mobile applications, or manipulating over the air (OTA) updates. To date, attackers can intercept vehicle data, issue commands, or track fleets in real time. Moreover, telematics companion apps for drivers have been found using hardcoded credentials, weak encryption, or unvalidated input, allowing unauthorized access. Finally, poorly protected update mechanisms may be spoofed or replayed, leading to arbitrary code execution on Telematics Control Units, TCUs or other vehicle computers. These issues illustrate that the digitalization of transport, while bringing undeniable operational benefits, also opens new attack surfaces that require continuous monitoring and improvement.

The above issues also indicate the importance of supply chain security and third-party risk. Therefore, ensuring cybersecurity in telematics is not a one-time effort but a dynamic, ongoing process that must evolve in parallel with technological progress and emerging threats. Cloud service providers, IoT device vendors, and software integrators all play critical roles in telematics security. Thus, a single unpatched vulnerability in a third-party module (e.g. an open-source MQTT broker or GPS library) can affect thousands of deployments. Incidents like the SolarWinds massive cyberattack in 2020, or the Log4Shell vulnerability discovery in 2021, and its exploitation by cybercriminals to attack a US federal agency in 2022, highlight the need for deep visibility into software supply chains in developing secure systems. As the vulnerabilities of telematics systems appear, the regulatory and compliance pressure is increasing. For example, the EU NIS2 Directive mandates reporting and resilience requirements for transport and logistics; UNECE R155 and R156 embed cybersecurity and software-update requirements into vehicle type approval – binding for manufacturers, but increasingly scrutinized by operators and insurers as well. Insurance markets are also beginning to demand proof of cyber risk management – cyber insurance premiums and exclusions are being updated to reflect real-time telemetry exposure.

The organizational weaknesses however remain, including siloed responsibility, limited cyber maturity, and underinvestment in human resources. First, the security ownership is often split between IT (Information Technology that deals with data processing and data management), and OT (Operational Technology that deals with process and devices monitoring and control), vehicle fleet, and external service providers. This often results in coverage gaps. Secondly, many mid-sized operators lack a formal cyber risk register, let alone a SOC. Patching, monitoring, and incident response are often ad hoc, or reactive, when an incident happens. Thirdly, frontline staff such as drivers, dispatchers, depot technicians, are rarely trained in cybersecurity basics relevant to telematics (e.g. secure Bluetooth pairing, hotspot risks, device tampering).

Telematic systems are not future risks – they are current attack surfaces. While large operators are beginning to integrate security-by-design, the broader ecosystem remains fragmented. Attackers already exploit these gaps. A clear understanding of today's threat landscape is essential for prioritizing controls, planning budgets, and avoiding costly incidents. Therefore, building a culture of cybersecurity awareness across all levels of transport organizations becomes crucial. This involves not only implementing technical safeguards but also fostering cooperation between system developers, operators, and policymakers to establish consistent standards and proactive defence mechanisms. Only such a holistic approach can ensure the resilience and long-term stability of telematics infrastructure in an increasingly digitalized transport environment.

4.4 Threats for Exploitation of Telematics Systems

While traditional transport risks involve physical hazards – collisions, breakdowns, delays, equipment usage – modern telematic systems introduce a new threat vector that is digital compromise. Attacks on these systems can undermine safety, privacy, operational continuity, and even national security. The common identified threat categories are presented in Table 4.6.

Telematic systems are vulnerable at multiple layers – from mobile apps and cloud dashboards to embedded vehicle components and road-side units. Attackers exploit not just technical flaws but organizational

Table 4.6 Threat Categories and Attack Paths

THREAT CATEGORY	EXAMPLE
Remote code execution (RCE)	Exploiting insecure OTA updates, vulnerable backend APIs, or improperly sandboxed TCU firmware.
Spoofing & impersonation	Faking vehicle identity in V2X communications to mislead other road users or infrastructure systems.
Data exfiltration	Accessing and leaking sensitive GPS, cargo, or driver behaviour data via weak cloud security or app flaws.
Denial of Service (DoS)	Disrupting vehicle communications or immobilizing fleets by flooding interfaces, jamming signals, or exhausting system resources.
Privilege escalation	Gaining elevated access on in-vehicle networks (e.g. from infotainment to CAN bus) through misconfigured access controls.
Attack	Exploit TCU firmware vulnerability via cellular connection.
	Credential stuffing or API abuse using leaked admin passwords.
	Tampering with RSU firmware to send falsified messages or disrupt signal prioritization.
	Reverse-engineering app to extract hardcoded API keys or access tokens.
Impact	Remote takeover of vehicle telemetry or diagnostics, unauthorized ECU commands, location spoofing.
	Real-time access to hundreds of vehicles, route history, fuel usage, and driver biometrics.
	Traffic chaos, potential collisions, revenue loss from toll misreporting.
	Unauthorized access to telematics backend services and personal data.

Source: Own elaboration.

blind spots. Understanding the how of system exploitation is essential to building effective detection, defence, and response strategies.

It is worth noting, that telematics abuse is not always external. Internal actors (drivers, contractors, maintenance staff) may also disable tracking to engage in unauthorized activities, sell access to fleet tracking systems or credentials. or insert USB-based malware during diagnostics or repair work. Detection of such cases is difficult unless system baselines and audit logs are actively monitored.

Attacks often begin outside the transport domain. A compromised email that requires providing sensitive data, and through VPN access can connect to fleet management server and TCU fleet or third-party vendor compromise (shared credentials and cloud dashboard). Such attacks emphasize the need for zero-trust principles, network segmentation, and secure supplier access.

It is important to mention the emerging threats, such as AI-based spoofing, cryptography risks, or vehicle swarm manipulation.

(i) AI-based spoofing: Generative AI can mimic driver behaviour, sensor signals, or system logs, obscuring real attacks;
(ii) Quantum-era cryptography risks: Future quantum computing could compromise long-term integrity of V2X signed messages or archived vehicle logs unless post-quantum algorithms are adopted;
(iii) Vehicle swarm manipulation: Coordinated manipulation of V2V/V2X messages across a fleet (e.g. platooning trucks) could result in synchronized disruptions or collisions.

Telematic systems are vulnerable at multiple layers – from mobile apps and cloud dashboards to embedded vehicle components and roadside units. Attackers exploit not just technical flaws, but organizational blind spots. Understanding how system exploitation is essential to building effective detection, defence, and response strategies.

4.5 Methods of Analysing Systems' Security

Understanding the security condition of a telematic system requires more than a one-time audit. It demands continuous, methodical analysis: spanning design, implementation, deployment, and operation.

Effective security analysis is not a one-time event – it's a continuous cycle of identifying risks, validating controls, and detecting anomalies. Operators should adopt a layered approach: threat modelling during design, penetration testing before deployment, and real-time monitoring during operations. Security assurance must be built into every phase of the telematic system lifecycle.

4.5.1 Threat Analysis and Risk Assessment (TARA)

TARA is a structured process for identifying potential threats, evaluating their likelihood and impact, and prioritizing mitigation actions. It is required by ISO/SAE 21434 for vehicle cybersecurity engineering. Also aligns with ISO 31000 and ISO/IEC 27005 principles. During vehicle system design, it helps assess which car computers electronic control units (ECUs) are most exposed (e.g. telematics gateway, infotainment). It also helps define cybersecurity goals early. Key techniques used in TARA include asset identification and impact rating, threat scenario identification, attack path analysis, as well as risk determination and treatment. These techniques are used to systematically identify potential cybersecurity threats and assess the associated risks, ultimately leading to mitigation strategies.

4.5.2 Vulnerability Assessments and Penetration Testing

These methods encompass vulnerability scanning, penetration testing, as well as fuzz testing. Vulnerability scanning is used to identify known flaws in telematics servers, mobile apps, vehicle firmware, etc., using tools like Nessus or OpenVAS. Penetration testing (pen-testing) is utilized to simulate real-world attacks on telematics infrastructure – e.g. exploiting an API to gain backend access or hijacking a GPS signal. Finally, fuzz testing is applied to send random or malformed data to components (especially vehicle ECUs) to uncover crash conditions or unintended behaviour. These are especially effective in pre-deployment testing of new fleet platforms, RSUs, or apps. However, they must be repeated regularly, particularly after updates or configuration changes.

4.5.3 Architecture Reviews and Security Audits

In this group of analysis types one can mention architecture review, audit against standards as well as gap analysis. Architecture review is a type of analysis that identifies system-wide weaknesses in design – e.g. flat networks, insecure update paths, unsegmented wireless access. It is important to mention that transport operators planning digital transformation or fleet modernization should run an architecture review before onboarding major telematics solutions. An audit against standards typically compares system controls to frameworks and international standards (e.g. ISO 27001, UNECE R155, or IEC 62443). It can be carried out internally, or by third parties. The gap analysis highlights misalignments between current practice and a given mandatory compliance (e.g. NIS2 reporting obligations).

4.5.4 Security Monitoring and Telemetry Analysis

The set of practices in this area encompasses Security Information and Event Management (SIEM), Intrusion Detection Systems (IDS) as well as detecting telematics anomalies. SIEM collects and correlates logs from telematics servers, cloud APIs, mobile apps, and network infrastructure to identify any anomalies or discrepancies. IDS monitor for abnormal patterns – e.g. sudden bursts of TCU commands or unauthorized firmware uploads. Telematics anomaly detection is based on specialized machine learning tools that flag unusual vehicle behaviour (e.g. engine diagnostics manipulation, GPS jamming). Monitoring is essential for post-deployment security – especially in meeting requirements under international standards.

4.5.5 Simulations

In order to test the system security, a controlled, adversary-style attack exercise designed to test the full incident detection and response capabilities of a transport organization can be carried out occasionally. It can simulate lateral movement from IT to OT environments, insider threats, or GPS spoofing across a vehicle fleet. It can also help validate runbooks, SOC procedures, and business continuity plans under stress, or sudden unexpected situations and crises being a result of cybersecurity breach.

Effective security analysis is not a one-time event – it is a continuous cycle of identifying risks, validating controls, and detecting anomalies. Operators should adopt a layered approach: threat modelling during design, penetration testing before deployment, and real-time monitoring during operations. Security assurance must be built into every phase of the telematic system lifecycle.

4.6 Securing Transport Telematic Systems in Practice

Translating cybersecurity into daily transport operations is where many organizations struggle. Standards, risk models, and audits are essential, but without practical implementation, even the most robust framework fails.

Security is not just a technical challenge – it is an operational discipline. Telematic systems must be secured across their life cycle, from procurement and deployment to day-to-day monitoring. Transport leaders must champion this integration, ensuring cybersecurity becomes part of safety, maintenance, and performance conversations. This requires embedding security principles into every organizational process, from staff training and incident response planning to supplier management and regulatory compliance. Only by treating cybersecurity as a strategic priority rather than a supplementary function can transport enterprises ensure the reliability, resilience, and long-term sustainability of their telematic infrastructures in an increasingly interconnected environment.

Securing transport telematic systems in practice can be based on the following pillars: (a) proper organizational design, (b) system and device security, (c) monitoring and continuous improvement.

4.6.1 Proper Organizational Design

Proper organizational design should offer a context, where strategic potential and effectively orchestrated resources will result in desired outcomes, such as higher level of system security. The organizational context assuring security requires both tight and loose structures

(Dyduch, 2019, pp. 65–82). Tight, centralized, bureaucratic structures facilitate the implementation of the strategic plan, assure that systems and procedures work flawlessly, whereas loose, organic, decentralized structures allow fast reaction to unexpected situations, and innovative approaches to problem solving.

Strategic design of an effective organization needs to encompass the following features:: (a) strong but adaptative organizational culture, that on one hand integrates and unifies the organization around common values and beliefs, but on the other hand allows it to adopt to changes and test new approaches in improving security; (b) proper organizational climate, where employees trust each other and work for a common strength; (c) knowledge management environment that leaves room for idea exchange, (d) flexible approach to change and introducing security corrective measures.

4.6.2 System and Device Security

Security of the telematics systems must align with what matters most for the organization, specifically: (a) operational continuity, (b) safety of personnel and passengers, (c) compliance with transport and data regulations, (d) reputation and customer trust.

The security of the telematic system can be wrapped around the following recommendations:

- Start with a risk register that connects assets (e.g. TCU, depot Wi-Fi, fleet portal) to business impacts. Use this to prioritize security investments.
- Require ISO/SAE 21434 or IEC 62443 conformity, evidence of threat modelling, and software bill of materials (SBOM).
- Include patch timelines, vulnerability disclosure policies, secure update mechanisms, and audit rights.
- Conduct penetration testing or configuration review before full rollout of telematic solutions.
- Only allow signed firmware, disable debug ports, segment internal networks, monitor diagnostics.
- Enforce MDM policies, prevent sideloading of apps, auto-wipe if lost/stolen, enforce app-level PINs.

- Segment wireless and telematics networks from office IT; harden roadside units using IEC 62443 guidelines.

4.6.3 Monitoring and Improvement

To monitor the telematic systems' security it is worth to develop a SOC. It may be internal or outsourced; it should ingest logs from telematics platforms, vehicle APIs, RSUs, and mobile endpoints. Another recommendation is to develop threat detection rules, and flag behaviours such as command replay, location spoofing, abnormal update schedules, or rapid logins across regions. Companies should have an incident response plan developed, and define the steps in case of security breach, hacking, etc. It is worth defining containment steps (e.g. isolate vehicle), communication protocols (internal + regulator), and data recovery procedures. In order to test the unpredicted situations, and to see whether an organization has ready procedures and can react promptly to risks, it is recommended to develop drills and table-top situations, that can be realized by simulating a telematics breach (e.g. OTA compromise or app hijack) and testing real-time coordination between operations and IT.

To continuously improve the system, four areas of action are required: post-event reviews, security metrics, compliance audits, and supplier reviews:

- Post-event reviews: After any cyber incident or near miss, perform a root cause analysis and update controls accordingly.
- Security metrics: Track patch rates, failed login attempts, incident response times, and user-reporting behaviour.
- Compliance audits: Prepare for UNECE R155, ISO 27001, and NIS2 by maintaining updated documentation and evidence of controls in action.
- Supplier reviews: Reassess third-party vendors annually or after any major software update or security incident.

To maintain the security of telematics system, the overall organizational culture of security needs to be developed. That includes (a) training drivers for phishing awareness, safe app/device use, or recognizing signs of compromise; (b) securing access to portals, regular password hygiene, anomaly reporting by logistics coordinators; (c) avoiding unauthorized USB devices, secure firmware updates, physical asset protection.

Securing telematic systems is not optional – it is strategically essential. As transport networks evolve into fully connected digital ecosystems, the threats grow more complex, and the consequences of failure more severe. By grounding cybersecurity in standards, understanding current threats, analysing system vulnerabilities, and executing practical defences, transport managers can ensure both resilience and trust in the systems they rely on every day.

References

Apache Foundation / MITRE (2021), Log4Shell Vulnerability (CVE-2021-44228).

Chudziński, P., Cyfert, S., Dyduch, W., Zastempowski, M. (2022), Risk management during the Covid-19 crisis: Business responses in the polish water utilities, *Journal of Water Supply Research and Technology-Aqua*, vol. 71, no. 3, 387–400.

Dyduch, W. (2019), Entrepreneurial strategy simulating value creation: Conceptual findings and some empirical tests, *Entrepreneurial Business and Economics Review*, vol. 7, no. 3, 139–159.

Engemann, K.J. (2019), Emerging developments in organizational risk, *Continuity & Resilience Review*, vol. 1, no. 11, 26–35.

ETSI EN 303 645 / ETSI TS 103 645 – Cyber Security for Consumer Internet of Things: Baseline Requirements. European Telecommunications Standards Institute.

Hoyt, R.E., Liebenberg, A.P. (2011), The value of enterprise risk management, *Journal of Risk and Insurance*, vol. 78, no. 4, 795–822.

IEEE Standards Association (2025), IEEE 1609.2 – Standard for Wireless Access in Vehicular Environments – Security Services for Applications and Management Messages.

International Electrotechnical Commission (2025), IEC 62443 Series – Industrial communication networks – Network and system security for industrial automation and control systems.

International Organization for Standardization (2025), ISO/IEC 5055:2021 – Software Engineering – Software quality measurement – Automated source code quality measures.

International Organization for Standardization (2025), ISO/IEC 27001:2022 – Information security, cybersecurity and privacy protection – Information security management systems – Requirements.

International Organization for Standardization (2025), ISO 26262:2018 – Road vehicles – Functional safety.

International Organization for Standardization (2025), ISO 31000:2018 – Risk management – Guidelines.

ISO and SAE International (2025), ISO/SAE 21434:2021 – Road vehicles – Cybersecurity engineering.

Król, A., Rokicki, T. (2021), Telematyka w zarządzaniu flotą samochodową, *Ekonomika i Organizacja Logistyki*, vol. 6, no. 4, 49–57.

Kurek, M. (2025), Od cyberpaniki do cyberstrategii, *MIT Sloan Management Review Polska*, no. 30, 1–15.

Marlow, D.R., Beale, D.J., Cook, S., Sharma, A. (2015), Investing in the water infrastructure of tomorrow, *Global Issues in Water Policy*, vol. 15, 217–236.

National Institute of Standards and Technology (2024), (CSF) NIST Cybersecurity Framework, Version 2.0 – Framework for Improving Critical Infrastructure Cybersecurity..

SAE J3061:2016 – Cybersecurity Guidebook for Cyber-Physical Vehicle Systems. SAE International.

Security Agency (CISA) (2020), SolarWinds Orion Breach Report. U.S. Cybersecurity and Infrastructure.

Targowski, A. (2023), *Informatyka strategiczna w dobie powszechnej cyfryzacji w XXI wieku*, Kraków: Polska Akademia Umiejętności.

United Nations Economic Commission for Europe. UNECE Regulation No. 155 – Uniform provisions concerning the approval of vehicles with regards to cyber security and cyber security management system.

United Nations Economic Commission for Europe. UNECE Regulation No. 156 – Software update processes and software update management systems for vehicles.

Summary

The monograph *Security Strategy of Intelligent Transport's Telematic Systems* returns to the fundamental premise outlined in the introduction: that transport, as one of the pillars of modern civilization, cannot evolve effectively without the deliberate and secure integration of advanced telematics and digital management systems. Nowadays, telematics is an essential way to improve safety and reliability of transport systems, enabling optimizing motion routes and reducing costs (Neumann, 2018, p. 617). At the same time, the dynamic development of intelligent transport requires not only innovative technological solutions but also strategic foresight, organizational adaptation, and the continuous enhancement of safety frameworks. The reflections and analyses presented throughout the chapters demonstrate that security must accompany progress at every stage of technological transformation – from the design of transport infrastructure to the implementation and operation of telematic systems.

The synthesis of theoretical and practical perspectives presented in this study confirms that the digitalization of transport processes has become both an opportunity and a challenge. On the one hand, intelligent telematics allows for optimization, automation and greater environmental sustainability. On the other, it introduces new risks and dependencies, particularly in the realm of data security, system integrity, and user awareness. "The introduction of technologies such as process automation, artificial intelligence, the Internet of Things, and cloud technologies opens up new opportunities for the industry, but these innovations may face certain threats at different stages of projects" (Zaiats & Oliinyk, 2024, p. 71). In this sense, transport management strategies must evolve from reactive to proactive, integrating cybersecurity considerations as an inherent component of organizational policy and strategic planning.

Furthermore, the book highlights that the efficiency of modern transport systems is inseparable from cooperation – between enterprises, public institutions, and technology providers. The development of

DOI: 10.1201/9781003646518-6

secure and intelligent mobility networks calls for interdisciplinary collaboration, harmonization of standards, and a shared commitment to building trust in the digital transport ecosystem. As the authors have shown, the future of transport will increasingly depend on how effectively safety mechanisms are embedded in the design and governance of telematic systems, rather than treated as a separate, final stage of development.

The conclusions drawn from this work reaffirm that the implementation of safe and intelligent transport telematics is not merely a technical necessity but a strategic imperative that affects the quality of life, economic competitiveness, and environmental balance. The authors' comprehensive approach, combining conceptual insights with practical recommendations, provides a valuable foundation for policymakers, researchers, and practitioners seeking to guide the transport sector toward sustainable digital maturity.

Ultimately, this monograph serves not only as a summary of current knowledge but also as a call to continue the scientific and professional dialogue on how to balance innovation with responsibility. By deepening understanding of the interplay between technology, management, and safety, it paves the way for the creation of a transport system that is not only efficient and intelligent but also resilient, ethical as well as human and nature-cantered (sustainable). Such an approach ensures that innovation serves the broader goals of social welfare and environmental stewardship, rather than technological progress alone. It also highlights the necessity of designing transport ecosystems that respect human values, promote inclusivity, and minimize the ecological footprint of mobility in the decades to come.

References

Neumann T. (2018), The importance of telematics in the transport system, *TransNav. The International Journal on Marine Navigation and Safety of Sea Transportation,* vol. 12, no. 3.

Zaiats O., Oliinyk A. (2024), Risks of digital transformation in road transportation projects, *Management of Development of Complex Systems*, vol. 60, 71–78.

Index

For Product Safety Concerns and Information please contact our EU representative GPSR@taylorandfrancis.com Taylor & Francis Verlag GmbH, Kaufingerstraße 24, 80331 München, Germany